HAITI

LAND OF INEQUALITY

HAITI

LAND OF INEQUALITY

by Mary C. Turck

Lerner Publications Company / Minneapolis

Website address: www.lernerbooks.com

All maps by Philip Schwartzberg, Meridian Mapping, Minneapolis.
Cover photo by © AP/Wide World Photos
Table of Contents photos (from top to bottom) by © U.S. Coast Guard—District Seven;
© Schomburg Center/Astor, Lenox, and Tilden Foundations; From "World's Work Magazine,"
courtesy of Sojourner Truth Library; © Carol Halebian; © Carol Halebian.

Series Consultant: Andrew Bell-Fialkoff
Editorial Director: Mary M. Rodgers
Editors: Natan Paradise and Martha Kranes
Designer: Michael Tacheny
Photo Researcher: Cheryl Hulting

LIBRARY OF CONGRESS CATALOGING-IN-PUBLICATION DATA

Turck, Mary C.
   Haiti : land of inequality / by Mary C. Turck
      p. cm. — (World in conflict)
   Includes bibliographical references and index.
   Summary: Examines the history of Haiti's ethnic conflict and its continuing effect
on the people of that country.
   ISBN 0–8225–3554–8 (lib. bdg. : alk. paper)
   1. Haiti—History—Juvenile literature. 2. Social conflict—Haiti—Juvenile
literature. [1. Haiti—History.] I. Title. II. Series.
F1915.2.B53 1999
972.94–dc21   97–44187

Manufactured in the United States of America
1 2 3 4 5 6 – JR – 04 03 02 01 00 99

CONTENTS

ABOUT THIS SERIES

Government firepower kills 25 protesters . . . . Thousands of refugees flee the country . . . . Rebels attack capital . . . . Racism and rage flare . . . . Fighting breaks out . . . . Peace talks stall . . . . Bombing toll rises to 52 . . . . Slaughter has cost up to 50,000 lives.

Conflicts between people occur across the globe, and we hear about some of the more spectacular and horrific episodes in the news. But since most fighting doesn't directly affect us, we often choose to ignore it. And even if we do take the time to learn about these conflicts—from newspapers, magazines, television news, or radio—we're often left with just a snapshot of the conflict instead of the whole reel of film.

Most news accounts don't tell you the whole story about a conflict, focusing instead on the attention-grabbing events that make the headlines. In addition, news sources may have a preconceived idea about who is right and who is wrong in a conflict. The stories that result often portray one side as the "bad guys" and the other as the "good guys."

The *World in Conflict* series approaches each conflict with the idea that wars and political disputes aren't simply about bullies and victims. Conflicts are complex problems that can often be traced back hundreds of years. The people fighting one another have complicated reasons for doing so. Fighting erupts between groups divided by ethnicity, religion, and nationalism. These groups fight over power, money, territory, control. Sometimes people who just want to go about their own business get caught up in a conflict just because they're there.

These books examine major conflicts around the world, some of which are very bloody and others that haven't involved a lot of violence. They portray the people involved in and affected by conflicts. They describe how each conflict got started, how it developed, and where it stands. The books also outline some of the ways people have tried to end the conflicts. By reading the stories behind the headlines, you will learn some reasons why people hate and fight one another and, in addition, why some people struggle so hard to end conflicts.

WORDS YOU NEED TO KNOW

amnesty: Safety granted by a government or other authority to a person or group found guilty of committing political crimes.

asylum: Protection, usually in a foreign country, granted to criminals or to political refugees where they are safe from retaliation or punishment.

bureaucrat: A member of a bureaucracy—a form of government that operates by a specific set of procedures directed by a hierarchy of authority. All government business must be conducted by the rules outlined by the administration.

coup d'état: French words meaning "blow to the state" that refer to a swift, sudden overthrow of a government.

de facto **government:** Meaning "government in fact," an acting authority that may have gained control of a region without going through proper, legal channels.

democratic: Describing a form of government in which a majority of the people or representatives chosen by the majority elect public officials. All decisions made by the government are ratified, or approved, by the people or by their representatives.

dictator: A person who comes to power and holds absolute authority over a territory for an indefinite amount of time, making all economic, military, and political decisions. A dictator typically rules with brutality, oppression, and suppression of the opposition.

embargo: A governmental decree prohibiting trade and transportation links to a particular place. An embargo, also called an **economic sanction,** is intended to warn or punish a particular group or to force by economic means an adversary to comply with the government's wishes.

fermage: A French word meaning "rent," that especially refers to rents paid for farmland. In Haiti army officers could lease farmland, which was worked by slaves. The officers made money off of the land and paid a portion of the money to the government.

guerrilla: A rebel fighter, usually not associated with an internationally recognized government, who engages in irregular warfare. Membership in a guerrilla group usually indicates radical, aggressive, or unconventional activities.

justice of the peace: A judge given the authority to oversee minor court cases and to commit offenders for trial.

paramilitary: Describing a supplementary fighting force. Often, but not always, this term is used to describe underground, illegal groups. Sometimes an illegal paramilitary group may support, through the use of violence, the current government and its policies. The aim of other paramilitary groups is the overthrow of the government.

privatize: To turn a business from state management or operation to private ownership.

refugee status: The legal ranking by which a person fleeing his or her homeland may be considered for immigration to another country. Conditions for attaining refugee status include occasions when a government is unable or unwilling to provide protection to its citizens against persecution and cruel treatment based upon race, ethnic background, religion, or political beliefs.

FOREWORD

by Andrew Bell-Fialkoff

Conflicts between various groups are as old as time. Peoples and tribes around the world have fought one another for thousands of years. In fact our history is in great part a succession of wars—between the Greeks and the Persians, the English and the French, the Russians and the Poles, and many others. Not only do states or ethnic groups fight one another, so do followers of different religions—Catholics and Protestants in Northern Ireland, Christians and Muslims in Bosnia, and Buddhists and Hindus in Sri Lanka. Often ethnicity, language, and religion—some of the main distinguishing elements of culture—reinforce one another in characterizing a particular group. For instance, the vast majority of Greeks are Orthodox Christian and speak Greek; most Italians are Roman Catholic and speak Italian. Elsewhere, one cultural aspect predominates. Serbs and Croats speak dialects of the same language but remain separate from one another because most Croats are Catholics and most Serbs are Orthodox Christians. To those two groups, religion is more important than language in defining culture.

We have witnessed an increasing number of conflicts in modern times—why? Three reasons stand out. One is that large empires—such as Austria-Hungary, Ottoman Turkey, several colonial empires with vast holdings in Asia, Africa, and America, and, most recently, the Soviet Union—have collapsed. A look at world maps from 1900, 1950, and 1998 reveals an ever-increasing number of small and medium-sized states. While empires existed, their rulers suppressed many ethnic and religious conflicts. Empires imposed order, and local resentments were mostly directed at the central authority. Inside the borders of empires, populations were multiethnic and often highly mixed. When the empires fell apart, world leaders found it impossible to establish political frontiers that coincided with ethnic boundaries. Different groups often claimed territories inhabited by others. The nations created on the lands of a toppled empire were saddled with acute border and ethnic problems from their very beginnings.

The second reason for more conflicts in modern times stems from the twin ideals of freedom and equality. In the United States, we usually think of freedom as "individual freedom." If we all have equal rights, we are free. But if you are a member of a minority group and feel that you are being discriminated against, your group's rights and freedoms are also important to you. In fact, if you don't have your "group freedom," you don't have full individual freedom either.

After World War I (1914–1918), the allied western nations, under the guidance of U.S. president Woodrow Wilson, tried to satisfy group rights by promoting minority rights. The spread of frantic nationalism in the 1930s, especially among disaffected ethnic minorities, and the catastrophe of World War II (1939–1945) led to a fundamental reassessment of the Wilsonian philosophy. After 1945 group rights were downplayed on the assumption that guaranteeing individual rights would be sufficient. In later decades, the collapse of multiethnic nations like Czechoslovakia, Yugoslavia, and the Soviet Union—coupled with the spread of nationalism in those regions—came as a shock to world leaders. People want democracy and individual rights, but they want their group rights, too. In practice, this means more conflicts and a cycle of secession, as minority ethnic groups seek their own sovereignty and independence.

The fires of conflict are often further stoked by the media, which lavishes glory and attention on independence movements. To fight for freedom is an honor. For every Palestinian who has killed an Israeli, there are hundreds of Kashmiris, Tamils, and Bosnians eager to shoot at their enemies. Newspapers, television and radio news broadcasts, and other media play a vital part in fomenting that sense of honor. They magnify each crisis, glorify rebellion, and help to feed the fire of conflict.

The third factor behind increasing conflict in the world is the social and geographic mobility that modern society enjoys. We can move anywhere we want and can aspire—or so we believe—to be anything we wish. Every day the television tantalizingly dangles the prizes that life can offer. We all want our share. But increased mobility and ambition also mean increased competition, which leads to antagonism. Antagonism often fastens itself to ethnic, racial, or religious differences. If you are an inner-city African American and your local grocer happens to be Korean American, you may see that individual as different from yourself—an intruder—rather than as a person, a neighbor, or a grocer. This same feeling of "us" versus "them" has been part of many an ethnic conflict around the world.

Many conflicts have been contained—even solved—by wise, responsible leadership. But unfortunately, many politicians use citizens' discontent for their own ends. They incite hatred, manipulate voters, and mobilize people against their neighbors. The worst things happen when neighbor turns against neighbor. In Bosnia, in Rwanda, in Lebanon, and in countless other places, people who had lived and worked together and had even intermarried went on a rampage, killing, raping, and robbing one another with gusto. If the appalling carnage teaches us anything, it is that we should stop seeing one another as hostile competitors and enemies and accept one another as people. Most importantly, we should learn to understand why conflicts happen and how they can be prevented. That is why *World in Conflict* is so important—the books in this series will help you understand the history and inner dynamics of some of the most persistent conflicts of modern times. And understanding is the first step to prevention. ⊕

INTRODUCTION

Haiti occupies a land that was once the richest area in the Western Hemisphere. In the late eighteenth century, when Haiti was still a French colony, the land was so productive that most of the French fleet was devoted to Haitian trade. In fact, Haiti provided a great portion of the world's coffee and sugar at that time. Modern Haiti, however, is the poorest country in the Western Hemisphere.

Most Haitians struggle to find enough to eat each day. They live in run-down or cardboard houses, have little or no education, and suffer from disease and malnutrition. Many Haitians cannot find jobs, and even those who work do not earn enough to support their families.

Yet there is tremendous wealth in Haiti. A small portion of the population lives in luxurious homes, surrounded by security walls and protected by guard dogs. These wealthy Haitians have servants, drive expensive cars, and go to the best schools. Just one-half of 1 percent of Haiti's population earns 46 percent of the nation's income.

Autocratic governments that have developed in Haiti over the last three centuries have fostered and maintained the economic and social inequalities in Haiti. Periodically Haitian society erupts in a new round of violence, as different groups struggle for political power and for control of the country's resources.

© Carol Halebian

For centuries Haitian society has been sharply divided into rich and poor. Many residents of Cité Soliel (above), *a neighborhood in the capital of Port-au-Prince, don't have jobs, adequate food or housing, or access to safe drinking water.*

Facing page: *Haiti shares the island of Hispaniola with the Dominican Republic. The island's attractive position in the Caribbean and its plentiful natural resources made it a perfect stop for early European sailors.*

ATLANTIC OCEAN

CUBA

Guantánamo Bay Naval Station
30 miles to the west

Jean-Rabel

⊙ Cap-Haïtien

Gonaïves

H A I T I

Gulf of
Gonâve

C a h o s

Saint Marc

Artibonite R.

Artibonite Valley

Gonâve Island

PORT-AU-PRINCE
⊙ Petionville

DOMINICAN REPUBLIC

● Les Cayes

Jacmel

CARIBBEAN SEA

○ PORT-AU-PRINCE	Capital
⊙ Petionville	Major City
● Les Cayes	Minor City
HAITI	Country Name
– ·· – ·· –	International Border

over 3,000 feet
1,500 feet
1,000 feet
sea level

0   10   20   30   40   50 miles

0   10   20   30   40   50 kilometers

Yet, the same few families have governed from behind the scenes as each successive group seized authority. In addition, the international community has played a large role in creating and maintaining the power structure that still exists in Haiti.

THE LAND

Haiti occupies the western third of the Caribbean island of Hispaniola, which is shaped like the claw of a giant crab reaching west. The capital, Port-au-Prince, is centrally located where the two peninsulas that form the crab's pincers meet. Port-au-Prince is more than six times the size of the second major city, Cap-Haïtien. The other important towns are Gonaïves, Les Cayes, Pétionville, and Jacmel. Haiti's immediate neighbor to the east is the Dominican Republic, which takes up the rest of the island. Approximately 700 miles southeast of Florida, Haiti lies among the islands of Cuba, Jamaica, and Puerto Rico.

Haiti's land area is 10,579 square miles, and almost two-thirds of it is rugged and mountainous. Five mountain ranges divide the country into northern, central, and southern regions. More than 100 rivers drain into the Atlantic Ocean to the east and into the Caribbean Sea to the west. The most important river, flowing east to west through the center of the country, is the Artibonite.

Because of the steep terrain, but also because of limited fertility or locally limited rainfall, only about 20 percent of Haiti's land is considered suitable for farming. Nearly half of Haiti, however, is under cultivation. Major crops include coffee beans, mangoes, cotton, cacao, essential oils, bananas, tobacco, and rice.

About 500 years ago, mahogany, cedar, coconut palm, avocado, orange, and mango trees covered 75 percent of the land. But most of the trees have been cut for lumber or made into charcoal for cooking. Farmers continue to clear trees for fuel or to

Fields cling to the sides of Haiti's mountains. Steep terrain, rocky soil, and erosion hamper efforts to plant crops and contribute to the problems of feeding the nation.

© Kay Shaw

make way for their crops. As a result, less than 4 percent of the forest remains, and erosion is a huge problem. Without trees to hold the thin mountain soils in place, the island's heavy rains wash the land down the steep slopes and into the sea. Farming in unsuitable areas or working the land too intensively only contribute to the widespread erosion.

Haiti's tropical climate is mostly hot and humid. The average daily temperature is 80 degrees. A dry season lasts from November to March, with two rainy seasons from April to June and from August to October. Both rainfall and temperature, however, vary more with elevation than with the time of year. On the northeast side of a mountain, for example, annual rainfall may reach 100 inches, washing out roads and making travel difficult. On the coast, the annual rainfall may be no more than 20 inches, limiting the land's agricultural productivity. In many of the driest lowland areas, cactus and thornbush predominate.

Haiti is also located in the middle of the hurricane belt,

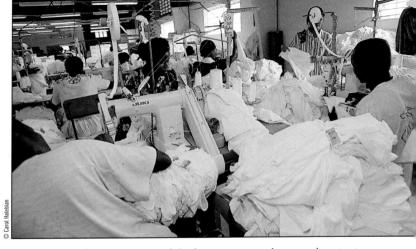
© Carol Halebian

Textile manufacturing is one of the few revenue-producing industries in Haiti. Many assembly plants opened in the 1970s, drawing rural people to the cities. But since then, political turmoil has forced many foreign-owned plants to close, leaving huge numbers of urbanites without jobs.

a region of the Atlantic and Caribbean waters where hurricanes are most likely to occur. Severe storms frequently buffet the island, and hurricanes periodically cause tremendous damage. In addition, Haiti is subject to earthquakes and periodic droughts. The country has had to rebuild repeatedly due to natural disasters, and this drain on the economy has taken a heavy toll on the Haitian people.

ECONOMIC CRISIS

Although Haiti is only about the size of Maryland, its population is estimated to be nearly 8 million people. The average population density is 618 people per square mile,

but with 2 million people living in Port-au-Prince, overpopulation is a major problem in the cities. Haiti does not have enough productive farmland to support its population. Most Haitians live in near-famine conditions, with close to a million people receiving food from private aid agencies.

Typically countries with inadequate agricultural resources try to develop other sectors of the economy to produce enough wealth to import food, but Haiti's industrial and service economies are extremely limited. In the 1970s, numerous foreign-owned assembly plants, especially U.S.-owned factories, opened in Haiti.

They attracted people from rural areas who could no longer support their families by farming the overworked land, and those who could not sell rice at low enough cost to compete with cheaper, imported rice. But political instability and increased regional competition, led to a decline in foreign investments in Haiti, leaving many Haitians jobless. Textile manufacturing and a limited number of assembly plants remain as the core of Haiti's industrial sector.

An almost complete absence of basic infrastructure for economic development serves as a significant barrier to foreign investment in Haiti. For example, less than 6 percent of the population has access to electrical

A woman collects water from a puddle in the sidewalk. Many urban Haitians must depend on unsafe sources of water, which they use for drinking, bathing, and cooking.

Statistics and Haiti

Most of the available statistics about modern Haiti are estimates. Current statistics in encyclopedias, almanacs, or similar sources, therefore, do not always agree. For example, some sources may list Haiti's population at close to 7 million, while others claim it is 8 million. According to some sources, only about 2 percent of Haiti remains forested, but other sources estimate 4 percent.

This statistical confusion is directly related to the political and economic crises in Haiti. One of the functions of government is to collect information about the country. In the United States, the government gathers economic statistics all the time, and a population census is taken every 10 years. This information is important both for the current allocation of resources and for future planning. But in Haiti, a combination of limited resources and governmental instability has meant that statistics are not collected regularly nor reliably. Most statistics about Haiti are based on estimates performed by governments or agencies outside Haiti, and these outside estimates can vary considerably.

In addition, conditions change in Haiti so quickly that many statistics are outdated almost as soon as they are estimated. In this book, therefore, statistics are generally given for the most recent year (as of publication) available.

power. Even in the capital, power is often available for only a few hours a day. Only eight people out of every thousand have telephone service. The few roads are mostly unpaved. There is no railroad. Nationwide, fewer than 13 percent of the population has access to safe drinking water.

Haiti's economic crisis is severe, and the standard of

living in Haiti is correspondingly low. In 1997 about 70 percent of Haiti's adult population was unemployed. Per capita income—the average amount of money earned by one person in one year—was less than $250, the lowest in the Western Hemisphere. In the same year, Haiti's infant mortality rate was more than 100 per 1,000 births, and the average life expectancy was less than 53 years. About 80 to 90 percent of all Haitians live in poverty and suffer from hunger and malnutrition.

A PEOPLE DIVIDED

Haitians are descended from European colonists and from West African slaves, who were imported to the island by the Spanish and the French in the seventeenth and eighteenth centuries. Haitians of mixed European and African ancestry are known as mulattoes. Although dark-skinned Haitians and mulattoes both live on the island, Haiti does not officially recognized these racial distinctions. According to the nation's 1804 constitution (drafted shortly after the country's independence from France), all Haitians are *noirs*. This term referred to

anyone faithful to the revolution, no matter what skin color.

But racial distinctions do matter in Haiti. Historically most of Haiti's wealthier families have been lighter-skinned mulattoes. Mulattoes—including those who migrated to the island in the nineteenth and twentieth centuries—continue to control much of the economic and political power in Haiti, even though they make up only about 5 percent of the population. The black major-

Wealthy Haitians flock to Haiti's beaches. Age-old socioeconomic classes that separate rich and poor have ensured the privileges of a modern-day Haitian elite.

ity, most of whom are poor, have often struggled with and have resented mulatto dominance.

Language, too, divides Haitians. Although both French and Creole are recognized as the official languages of Haiti, French is the language of power—the language taught in schools and learned by the children of the mulatto elite. In colonial days, French colonists often sent their children—including their mulatto children—to France for their education. These days French language and culture retain their dominant status. Until 1978 French was the only language allowed in schools, and until 1987 it was the only official language of Haiti. But only about 10 percent of the population speaks French.

Most Haitians speak Creole. Haitian Creole has a vocabulary that is mostly French in origin, but its grammar is highly characteristic of some African languages. Historically Creole has been the everyday language of all the people, regardless of social class, while French has been the formal language of schools, newspapers, official documents, the law, and the courts.

Voodoo

Voodoo is based on the religions of West Africa. The word *voodoo* comes from the Fon language of Benin and means "spirit." When Africans were imported to Haiti as slaves, they brought with them their beliefs in spirits who acted as intermediaries with a single god. Some of these spirits, or *loa,* were ancestors of the living. Others represented human emotions or forces of nature.

Colonial rulers forbade the slaves to practice their religion. The slaves were baptized as Roman Catholics and were severely punished for any refusal to adopt Catholicism. While outwardly accepting Christianity, the Africans combined Roman Catholic and African religious beliefs and practices, producing the religion known as voodoo. Practitioners of voodoo borrowed freely from Roman Catholic ritual, and tribal loa often took on the form of Catholic saints.

Voodoo ceremonies are characterized by singing, drumming, praying, feasting, offering gifts to the loa, and ritually sacrificing animals. Voodoo priests and priestesses also act as healers, counselors, and protectors against witchcraft.

© Carol Halebian

Through most of Haitian history, the Roman Catholic clergy tried to suppress voodoo. The Roman Catholic Church lately has become more tolerant of voodoo.

THE STRUGGLE FOR POWER

Since gaining independence from France in 1804, Haiti has been ruled, for the most part, by a series of **dictators** who have used the military to maintain their power. Whether the country's leadership has come from the mulatto elite or from the ranks of black military officers, the common factor has been strict authority over the lives of the country's black citizens.

The current cycle of conflict began with the overthrow of the Duvalier regime, a family of dictators who governed Haiti from 1957 to 1986. A series of transitional governments, with leaders emerging from the military, ruled Haiti until 1990, when Father Jean-Bertrand Aristide was elected president with the overwhelming support of the country's poor, black population. The election was widely considered to be the most **democratic** and fair election that Haiti had ever seen.

This language division has left the majority of Haitians unable to function in the educational and legal systems of their own country. Even though Creole is finally recognized as an official language of Haiti, its status among French speakers remains low.

Religion also divides Haitian society. About 80 percent of Haitians identify themselves as Roman Catholic, but most also practice voodoo, a mixture of Roman Catholic ritual elements and African religious beliefs and practices.

In October 1993, members of the Front pour l'Avancement et Progrès Haïtien (FRAPH)—a violent, pro-Duvalier group—protested the scheduled return of ousted president Jean-Bertrand Aristide. Displaying a poster of ex-president Jean-Claude "Baby Doc" Duvalier, FRAPH members show their support of the former regime.

Within a year of Aristide's election, however, the Haitian military staged a **coup d'état** to regain its control of the country. The military was supported by a number of violent **paramilitary** organizations. The Organization of American States (OAS, an alliance of countries in the Western Hemisphere), the United Nations (UN), and the United States intervened in an attempt to restore the democratically elected leader to power in Haiti. But only after three years of negotiations and economic **embargoes** did Aristide return to serve out the last year of his presidency.

Although Aristide was returned to power in 1994 and his successor, René Préval, became president in 1995, Haiti's ability to maintain a peaceful, democratic form of government remains in question. The country is faced with overwhelming economic, environmental, social, and political turmoil. The military leadership, the mulatto elite, and the black majority have yet to solve the problem. For most Haitians, every day is still a struggle just to survive. ⊕

MAJOR PLAYERS IN THE CONFLICT

Jean-Bertrand Aristide

Haiti

Emmanuel Constant

Aristide, Jean-Bertrand Roman Catholic priest and leader of the *lavalas* movement of the poor. Aristide was elected president of Haiti in 1990, was overthrown in a military coup in 1991, and was returned to the presidency for 1994 through 1995. In 1996 he created a new political party, the Lavalas Family.

Constant, Emmanuel Founder and head of FRAPH (Front pour l'Avancement et Progrès Haïtien), a violent paramilitary group that supported the 1991 military coup. He has resided in Queens, New York, since 1996 with permission of the U.S. government.

Haitian Military Historically the source of many of Haiti's leaders, and the strongest Haitian power since 1986. Aristide disbanded the military in 1995 and replaced it with a civilian police force.

Lavalas Family The political party formed by Aristide in 1996. In 1997 the OPL accused the Lavalas Family of electoral fraud. The feuding parties have been at a standoff ever since.

Organization of American States (OAS) A political alliance of 35 countries in the Western Hemisphere founded in 1948. The OAS imposed an embargo on Haiti after the military coup in 1991 and worked to negotiate Aristide's return to power. In 1993 the OAS joined the United Nations in establishing a civilian mission to monitor conditions in Haiti. After Aristide returned to power in 1994, the OAS helped supervise a return to democratic government.

Organization of the People in Struggle (OPL, formerly Lavalas Political Organization) The OPL, once part of the Lavalas coalition that elected both Presidents Aristide and Préval, controls the Haitian parliament and has maintained a political stalemate with Préval's administration since 1996. In 1997 the OPL charged Aristide's party, the Lavalas Family, with electoral fraud.

Préval, René Prime minister under President Aristide, he succeeded Aristide as president of Haiti in the 1995 elections.

United Nations (UN) A nongovernmental agency set up in 1945 to work for world peace. The UN took an active role in returning Aristide to power, including declaring an oil and arms embargo against Haiti and authorizing a multinational military presence in Haiti. The operation was known as the United Nations Mission in Haiti (UNMIH). In 1994 this multinational force, led by the United States, landed in Haiti and supervised the transition to democratic civilian rule.

United States Occupied Haiti from 1915 to 1934. The United States played a leading role, both militarily and diplomatically, in returning Aristide to Haiti. U.S. troops led the multinational force that landed in Haiti in 1994. Since 1995 the U.S. has phased out its military involvement in Haiti but continues to take an active role in pressing for economic changes.

OAS Emblem

René Préval

UN Emblem

CHAPTER

1

THE RECENT CONFLICT AND ITS EFFECTS

In 1990, after 186 years of dictatorship and military rule, Haitians voted in the country's first fully democratic elections. Father Jean-Bertrand Aristide won the 1990 presidential election by an overwhelming majority and was inaugurated as president of Haiti on February 7, 1991.

Aristide, 35 years old when he became president, had already spent nearly a decade as a Catholic priest in what Haitians call the Ti Legliz (Little Church, or the church of the poor). His experiences preaching in the impoverished neighborhoods of Port-au-Prince had convinced him of the need for social and economic reform. And most of his support in the election came from the poor, who make up the bulk of Haiti's population.

Thousands of people attended the February 7 inauguration of the young priest. President Aristide gave his inaugural address in Creole and welcomed beggars and poor people to the palace lawns for a feast. Recognizing the unlikelihood of reversing Haiti's economic situation overnight, President Aristide said his administration's immediate goal was to move the country "from misery to a dignified poverty."

© Carol Halebian

Aristide began his presidency by displaying his commitment to Haiti's poor. Hundreds of people flocked to the National Palace in support of Aristide for a symbolic feast, unprecedented in Haiti's years of elite or military rulers.

Jean-Bertrand Aristide

© Carol Halebian

Jean-Bertrand Aristide was born on July 15, 1953, in southwestern Haiti, where his family lived in a little house in the hills. After his father's death, the family moved to Port-au-Prince. The young Aristide returned often to visit his grandfather, who worked his land and shared his harvest. Aristide's grandfather greatly influenced the future president. For example, he defended poor people who stole potatoes to eat, telling the boy, "You cannot count the hairs in my beard, but you can count the people here who are suffering from injustice." Spending summers in the countryside, Aristide "saw there a people who had never succumbed to resignation. No matter how hard life was, or death, they tried to transform it."

As a young man, Aristide studied in Europe and in the Middle East before being ordained as a Roman Catholic priest in 1982. After preaching against the injustices of the Duvalier regime in his Port-au-Prince parish, Aristide was exiled to Montreal, Canada. He returned to Haiti in 1985 and participated in the popular movements that led to the end of the Duvalier regime in 1986.

Aristide spoke and acted on behalf of the poor. He preached about the dignity of all people and the mandate of Christians to stand in solidarity with the poor and the oppressed. His sermons denounced abusive military officials by name. He called capitalism a "mortal sin" because it favored the rich over the poor. He accused Haiti's wealthy class of betraying the country through a corrupt and criminal system.

Catholic leaders, most of whom came from the ranks of the economic elite, distrusted Aristide and feared the consequences of his preaching. The military also believed Aristide was a threat to the established order. Catholic leaders removed him from his parish. The military tried three times to kill him. On September 11, 1988, Aristide's church was torched during Mass, and more than a dozen people praying inside were murdered.

Aristide continued his struggle. "Together, together, we are *lavalas*." Lavalas, the Creole word for the heavy rainfall that sweeps down from the mountains and washes filth into the sea, became the name of Aristide's political movement. In 1990 Jean-Bertrand Aristide was elected president by 67 percent of the vote. The poor majority of Haitians welcomed the election as a second revolution.

To this end, Aristide's prime minister, René Préval, called upon the rich to share their wealth. He declared that the government's priorities would be to improve the nation's literacy rate, health care, agriculture, and the judicial system. Judicial reform included fighting corruption, creating a civilian police force independent of the army, and prosecuting those people responsible for political violence.

AP/Wide World Photos

Divisiveness, disorganization, and inexperience handicapped the new government, however. Aristide's proposals to double the minimum wage to $3.20 per day, to collect taxes (from which the elite had been traditionally exempt), and to cut prices were angrily rejected by the business community. International donors pledged almost half a billion dollars in aid, but Aristide's administration was slow to put together projects to use the money.

In addition, Aristide had many powerful opponents in

Haiti. The military leaders believed, with some reason, that Aristide meant to remove them from power and to greatly weaken the armed forces. The wealthy interpreted Aristide's speeches as encouraging violence against the rich and against political opposition. Many members of the Haitian legislature, moreover, were not supporters of Aristide. In August 1991, the legislature threatened a vote of no confidence in Prime Minister Préval. Massive popular demonstrations in support of Aristide

and Préval filled the streets, and rumors of an impending coup were common.

THE COUP

On the morning of September 30, 1991, President Aristide arrived at the National Palace, the seat of federal government in Port-au-Prince, to find that his presidential guard had disappeared. Lieutenant General Raoul Cédras, promoted to army chief of staff by Aristide in February, had turned against the president and had taken control of the government in

Facing page: *Four days after the 1991 coup, truckloads of soldiers and police patrolled the deserted streets of Port-au-Prince. Violence ensued as Aristide supporters objected to the removal of their elected leader after just nine months in office.*

a military coup d'état. Responding to pressure from the United States and from other countries, Cédras eventually allowed Aristide to flee to safety on a plane to Venezuela.

Many others were not so lucky. Military leaders and troops worried about having to give up their privileged lifestyles and feared retaliation from the poor majority for their oppression. In the next few weeks, members of the military and their supporters killed at least 1,000 Haitians, opponents of the coup and ordinary civilians. They beat, arrested, or tortured thousands of others. The army took over all tele-

The Brothers Izmery

Although most victims of anti-Aristide violence came from the poor neighborhoods that were home to most of the exiled president's supporters, wealthy backers were not immune. On May 26, 1992, Georges Izmery, a prosperous Port-au-Prince businessperson who was for Aristide, was crossing the street from his store to his car. Several gunmen opened fire and shot him down in the street. Although a police station was nearby, the police failed to pursue his attackers. Instead, they picked up the still-living Izmery from the street and carried him off to a hospital morgue, ignoring the pleas and protests of family members. No doctors were allowed to attend Izmery.

A few days later, Georges's brother Antoine spoke at his funeral. Antoine also was a supporter of the exiled president. He warned that "every honest person must reproach this intolerable situation or wait one day to be the next victim." Soldiers surrounded the cathedral during Georges's funeral, and the mourners, including Antoine, were beaten as they left. Soldiers attacked the funeral procession carrying Georges Izmery's body to the cemetery.

Antoine Izmery was arrested and jailed after meeting with U.S. activist Jesse Jackson in January 1993. International pressure led to Antoine's release. On September 11, 1993, anti-Aristide gunmen dragged Antoine Izmery out of a memorial service that he had organized in Port-au-Prince. They shot him in the street along with a witness to the murder.

vision and radio stations and shut down the offices of popular organizations. A favorite radio announcer was arrested, and his body was found two days later.

Cité Soleil, the poor Port-au-Prince neighborhood where Aristide experienced wide support, endured five days and nights of massacre. The military dumped many of the bodies in mass graves. As a result of the violence, tens of thousands of people fled the capital. Some hid in the countryside, while others left for the United States or for the neighboring Dominican Republic.

In carrying out the coup, Cédras had the support of Port-au-Prince police chief Colonel Joseph Michel François, who headed a 2,500-member military police force. In addition, Cédras and François controlled hundreds of attachés, or paramilitary auxiliary troops

---

[Aristide supporter] Jean-Claude Museau was forced to eat the photographs of Aristide that he had with him. He died, too, along with so many anonymous victims. . . .

---

in civilian clothes. Attachés used terror to instill fear, extract obedience, and enforce silence. The army routinely harassed journalists, human-rights observers, lawyers, students, priests, and grassroots leaders. But their chief targets were people with actual or supposed links to President Aristide.

In one incident of violence on December 6, 1992, soldiers took seven students to a military execution ground and shot them. Twenty-year-old Jean-Sony Philogène survived and managed to get to St. Francis de Sales hospital. Sensing danger, the doctor who treated him transferred the young student to Canapé Vert hospital. Soldiers found Philogène within hours of his transfer and shot the young man to death.

In another incident on February 25, 1993, parlimentary attachés beat Bishop Willy Romélus, human rights activist Paul Dejean, several journalists, and many others in attendance at a Mass at the National Cathedral in Port-au-Prince. The cathedral was surrounded by at least 100 men who attacked people trying to enter or leave the building. Groups of police officers stood around watching the beatings, then broke up each attack and removed the victim, leaving the attackers free to find new targets.

Colin Granderson and Michael Moeller (heads of an observer mission sent to Haiti by the UN and the OAS to report on the evolving conflict) attended the Mass and observed the violence outside. To ensure a safe exit for the parishioners, Moeller asked other diplomats in attendance to line up their cars in front of the building. When the cars were ready, Moeller sent people out in groups of three to be escorted to safety by the drivers. Bishop Romélus, a prominent critic of the military coup, refused to leave the church until his parishioners were safe. When he finally left, accompanied by supporters, about 20 attachés attacked him. French embassy officials finally rescued Romélus.

Less prominent Haitians suffered even more under the military regime, although their stories were less frequently recorded. At night attachés, soldiers, and paramilitary terrorized small villages. They rampaged through the streets, killing people and looting homes. Often the attachés and soldiers attacked people living in the slums of Port-au-Prince. When they could, slum dwellers fled to the countryside to escape. Any people who were known to have been politically active, or even to have known someone who was, were targets for harassment and violence.

EMBARGO AGAINST HAITI

A delegation from the OAS, which wished to see Aristide returned to power in Haiti, arrived in Port-au-Prince in 1991 to begin negotiations with the military and with other coup leaders. Soldiers harassed the delegates and Port-au-Prince mayor Evans Paul. The OAS called its delegates away. Convinced that the military regime would not negotiate, the OAS imposed a trade embargo against Haiti.

> *The main results of [the embargo] were the unbridled enrichment of a small minority that was already well off..., and the impoverishment of others....*

Meanwhile, the UN condemned the coup and announced that it would not recognize the new regime. With the notable exception of the Vatican, which recognized the **de facto government** in April 1992, most countries refused to acknowledge the Haitian government. The UN imposed a fuel and arms embargo against Haiti on June 16, 1993.

In theory, the combined OAS and UN embargoes were intended to stop all international trade with Haiti, thus pressuring the military regime to negotiate a return to the democratically elected government. In practice, the embargoes were ineffective.

Unable to afford the high price of gasoline, laborers use muscle to haul a cart laden with bags of flour uphill. The OAS and UN embargoes took their heaviest toll on Haiti's poor, while doing little to return Aristide to power.

AP/Wide World Photos

Haitian women wait in line for food distribution in Cité Soleil. Three years of sanctions made daily life in Haiti a struggle. Hundreds of thousands of people relied on international aid agencies to supply daily food rations.

Reuters/Lee Celano/Archive Photos

Although they did succeed in crippling Haiti's economy, those with money or political power escaped the worst effects, and the coup leaders felt no pressure to negotiate.

Since the neighboring Dominican Republic did not adhere to the embargo, wealthy Haitians suffered little. A road was built from Port-au-Prince to the Dominican Republic border. The rich were able to bring goods into Haiti or could arrange to route shipments through the Dominican Republic to Haiti. For instance, a Liberian tanker delivered four million gallons of fuel to a Shell dock near Port-au-Prince in November of 1991. Other tankers arrived the following January. This fuel was extremely expensive and did not arrive in large enough quantities to supply the needs of all Haitians. The wealthy had money to buy fuel for their cars, but the poor depended on buses, which often lacked fuel and which had to raise fares to compensate for the increase in oil prices.

Even those nations that agreed to observe an embargo against Haiti often enforced it inconsistently. The United States, for example, officially supported the OAS embargo. U.S. president George Bush signed a document banning all commerce with Haiti except for humanitarian aid, which included food and medicine. Just a few months later, however, the U.S. government modified the embargo to allow U.S. assembly plants in Haiti to continue trade with the United States. This decision allowed Haiti's business community to escape some of the effects of the embargo.

The poor suffered from the lack of fuel and from the high prices that smugglers charged for everyday goods. Medical officials estimated that at least 10,000 Haitians died during the first 18 months after the coup, many of them from severe malnutrition or from preventable diseases that resulted from hardships created by the trade embargoes. During the years that the embargoes were in place (1991–1994), Haiti's gross domestic product (a country's economic output in one year) decreased by about 40 percent. Inflation rose from 7 to 52 percent, while exports, imports, and agricultural production dropped. Employment in the assembly-for-export industries fell from 44,000 in 1991 to 8,000 in 1994. By mid-1993, more than 850,000 Haitians were dependent on international aid groups for daily meals, and more than half of the country's workforce was unemployed.

REFUGEE CRISIS

Tens of thousands of Haitians fled their homeland during the years following the coup. Many were driven by the fear of violence at the hands of the attachés and the military. Others were driven by economic pressure fueled by the embargo. To flee the island, refugees crowded into frail, leaky boats. Some refugees were killed by soldiers as they tried to leave. Hundreds more drowned at sea.

In earlier years, Haitians had fled terror and hardship at home by seeking refuge in the United States. Many middle-class Haitians had immigrated to the United States legally. Others, knowing that the United States was not

Hundreds of angry anti-embargo protestors mob the newly arrived OAS representatives. They had come to meet with military leaders to negotiate the return of Aristide to power.

AP/Wide World Photos

Haitian refugees climb aboard a U.S. Coast Guard vessel that intercepted them at sea. The United States returned many refugees to Haiti. It sent others to a refugee camp at the U.S. Naval base at Guantánamo Bay, Cuba.

granting Haitians **refugee status,** entered the United States illegally and remained as undocumented immigrants. Most refugees from the 1991 coup pointed their boats toward the United States.

On November 13, 1991, in accordance with U.S. policy at the time, the U.S. Coast Guard intercepted and forcibly returned to Haiti the first boatload of refugees to reach U.S. waters. During the following weeks, these Haitian refugees were met by Haitian police and officials, who fingerprinted and photographed them. Some were arrested on the spot. Others returned to their homes to be met with death threats.

Human-rights activists within the United States filed legal challenges against the Bush administration's policy of returning refugees to Haiti. In response, a federal district court judge temporarily halted the forced return of refugees. The U.S. government then set up a special camp at the U.S. military base in far-eastern Cuba at Guantánamo Bay.

Any Haitians picked up at sea were shipped to Guantánamo Bay, where they were held in refugee camps. By February 1992, when the U.S. Supreme Court overturned the ban on the forced return of refugees, more than 16,000 Haitian refugees had been picked up at sea.

In May 1992, President Bush signed an order directing the Coast Guard to stop all Haitian refugee boats and return their passengers immediately to Port-au-Prince. Despite this order, refugees continued to flee the country, taking to the sea in large numbers. The United States,

which feared a flood of refugees if it allowed Haitians to reach U.S. shores, then tried instituting "in-country" processing of refugee applications at the U.S. embassy in Port-au-Prince. Human-rights activists in the United States and in Haiti pointed out that Haitians who feared arrest and assassination could hardly be expected to appear at the U.S. embassy in full view of Haitian military personnel, apply for refuge, and then return home to wait for weeks or months for approval to emigrate. The refugee crisis continued.

MONTHS OF NEGOTIATION

Despite military-sponsored harassment and violence, Aristide's supporters continued to protest against Cédras and his military regime. Students, unions, and popular organizations coordinated a general strike on May 21, 1992. Protesters were held hostage by police and armed civilians in June and again in November. Three members of a pro-Aristide political party were shot dead in August as they put up Aristide posters.

In January 1993, Aristide wrote to the UN asking that the UN and the OAS deploy

From behind barbed-wire fences, refugees at Guantánamo Bay wait to find out if they will be allowed to enter the United States or if they will return to Haiti. Many feared for their safety if the United States sent them back to their homeland.

© Carol Halebian

Victims of politically motivated killings lay unburied. Despite efforts to resolve the conflict and to monitor human rights in Haiti, violence continued.

Reuters/Corbis-Bettmann

a civilian mission to monitor human-rights abuses. The first team of observers arrived in February. Meanwhile, the UN, the OAS, and the United States continued to try to resolve Haiti's political crisis by bringing Aristide and Cédras to the negotiating table. Several agreements were reached, but all were broken before their terms could be implemented. The UN-OAS human-rights observers left Haiti in October 1993 due to increasing danger. They reported an escalation of violence against the Haitian people.

By early 1994, Haiti had been devastated by years of violence, and the **economic sanctions** were taking an increasingly severe toll on the poor. More than 150,000 jobs had been lost since the 1991 coup, 40,000 of these in the assembly-for-export sector. More than half of the country's 2.8-million-person workforce was unemployed or underemployed. Education had been disrupted, and the country's already poor infrastructure had been all but destroyed. Hunger, disease, and death visited nearly every household.

After all efforts to negotiate a peaceful exit for the military leaders failed, the UN Security Council voted on July 31, 1994, to allow the United States to occupy Haiti in order to remove the military regime and to reinstate Aristide. Inside Haiti, some warned that, with a U.S. invasion, Aristide would become little more than a puppet in the hands of the United States. Others feared that Haiti would lose its sovereignty. But many were desperate for any resolution to the crisis.

Aristide's official stance on the invasion remained carefully ambiguous. To endorse a U.S. invasion would cost him the support of many Haitians. But there seemed no other way for him to return. On September 19, 1994, the United States invaded Haiti. Only when U.S. troops were on the way did Cédras agree to leave.

ARISTIDE RETURNS

A poor nation when Aristide was elected, Haiti was in far worse condition when he returned. Despite the wild celebrations that greeted the Haitian president, Aristide faced a difficult future. To secure international financial aid and loans to rebuild the country—but also as a condition for his return—President Aristide had to commit to economic reforms.

These measures, such as removing price controls (fixed, affordable prices) and laying off government workers, would inflict still more hardship on the poor. Many of these reforms were widely opposed within Haiti.

Nevertheless, Aristide's supporters urged him to seek

On September 19, 1994, a U.S.-led multinational force landed its first troops in Port-au-Prince. Although soldiers expected to be landing in hostile territory, they had received instructions from officers in charge to cooperate with the Haitian army. Haitian military leaders had been offered a deal by the United States if they agreed to leave peacefully and complied with the transfer of power back to Aristide.

Reuters/Jim Bourg/Archive Photos

Four months after Aristide's return to Haiti, his term was over. On February 7, 1996, he congratulated his successor, his former prime minister René Préval.

an extension of his presidential term to make up for the years of his absence. He refused. Instead, he moved the country toward the next presidential election. The candidate he backed, René Préval, won easily and was inaugurated as president in 1996.

Free elections do not fix problems overnight. Haiti is still poor. Farmers cannot support their families off the land, and immigrants from the countryside crowd into Port-au-Prince. There they compete with one another for low-paying jobs in foreign-owned assembly plants.

Although the military and the attachés no longer hold power, they have not been arrested and punished for their crimes. The United States and the UN promised to help create a new, professional police force. The new organization was to be independent of the military in Haiti. Nevertheless, many former members of police, military, and paramilitary groups managed to become part of the new police force.

The return to democratic government has not gone smoothly either. Haiti's legislature has been at odds with Préval, refusing to approve his economic plans. At issue is both genuine disagreement on the effect Préval's policies will have on the Haitian people as well as political maneuvering as Haiti's political parties prepare for upcoming elections. Meaningful legislation has fallen by the wayside. While the politicians refuse to compromise, foreign aid has been jeopardized, and the people's hopes have gone stale.

With the rising cost of living, many Haitians live in worse economic conditions than they did before the 1991 coup. And many people lost faith in the democratic process after watching the coup remove Aristide from office for most of his term. They saw international and domestic pressures force him to abandon the political and economic policies the people supported. In addition, Haitians feel that ballots no longer offer appealing choices. In the April 1997 elections for local and legislative offices, only 5 percent of the voters cast their ballots. Apathy and despair may pose a greater threat to democracy in Haiti than any coup. Haiti's future seems as uncertain as its past is bloody. ⊕

In 1998 the effects of Hurricane Georges were devastating. Nearly nine years after Haiti's first democratically elected president took office, little had changed economically for the majority of Haitians.

CHAPTER

2

THE CONFLICT'S ROOTS

When Christopher Columbus landed on the island of Hispaniola in 1492, it was home to the Arawak Indians. By 1550 this indigenous population had been almost entirely wiped out. Some had succumbed to European diseases, and others had died as slaves in the mines of Spanish colonial rulers. In their search for gold, the Spaniards imported West Africans to work as slaves. But the Spanish colony was not successful, and Spain soon came to neglect Hispaniola. However, a Spanish presence remained, mostly in central and eastern Hispaniola.

In 1629 the French gained their first foothold in the region on the island of Tortuga off the northwestern coast of Hispaniola. The French king Louis XIV commissioned the first permanent settlement on Tortuga in 1659. The settlers quickly colonized

An illustration shows the native population of what would become Hispaniola greeting Christopher Columbus and his crew on their first visit to the Caribbean island.

Corbis-Bettmann

Both Spanish and French settlers imported slaves to the island of Hispaniola to work on plantations.

Library of Congress

the northwestern part of Hispaniola as well, taking advantage of its remoteness from the Spanish capital of Santo Domingo. In 1664 the French West India Company was established to direct the expected commerce between France and its growing colony, and in 1670 France made Cap Français (modern Cap-Haïtien) its first major settlement on Hispaniola.

In 1695 the Treaty of Ryswick formally divided the island of Hispaniola between the French in the west and the Spaniards in the east. The French portion of the island was renamed Saint Domingue and later became Haiti, while the eastern part of the island was known as Santo Domingo until it became the independent Dominican Republic.

The French colonists in Saint Domingue built huge plantations, and by the mid-1700s almost 250,000 acres of sugar, coffee, cotton, and indigo (a plant used for making blue dye) had been planted. In 1767 the island exported 123 million pounds of sugar, 1 million pounds of indigo, 2 million pounds of coffee, as well as animal hides, molasses, cocoa, and rum. By 1789 about 1,000 merchant ships carried goods between Haiti and France, making up 67 percent of all French export and import trade.

To work these huge plantations, the French colonists, like the Spaniards before them, imported slaves from West Africa. The plantation owners' power over these slaves was absolute. All slaves were branded on the chest when purchased. Beatings and torture were everyday occurrences. Slaves

A white master with a whip oversees two slaves planting sugarcane. Slave labor enabled Saint Domingue's plantations to supply two-thirds of France's overseas trade.

Corbis-Bettmann

harvesting sugarcane were sometimes made to wear tin-plate masks to keep them from eating any of the cane. In fact, slaves were often required to raise their own food, using Sunday—their only free day—as the day to cultivate small plots of land.

The French, who were completely dependent on slave labor for their prosperity, worked many of the slaves to death. Although more than 1 million slaves had been shipped to Haiti by 1789, the population of the island was only a little over 500,000 people—39,000 whites, 27,000 mulattoes (known as *gens de couleur*), and 452,000 slaves.

EARLY SOCIAL DIVISIONS

Whites, gens de couleur, and slaves made up the three main social classes of Saint Domingue. But within these classes there were further divisions. In addition to the wealthy, white plantation owners, for example, Saint

to the colony as convicts. The rich whites scorned poor whites, and in early Saint Domingue, wealthy white men often preferred to marry mulatto women rather than poor white women. White military officers despised civilians, who returned the sentiment, and white townspeople could not agree with white plantation owners.

Similarly, some mulattoes were wealthy, had been educated in France, and owned property and slaves. In fact,

---

. . . so despised [were blacks] that even a Mulatto slave felt himself superior to the free black man. The Mulatto, rather than be [a] slave to a black, would have killed himself.

Domingue was populated by whites who came to the island from France as indentured servants (contracted help) or who were shipped

gens de couleur owned about a quarter of the slaves in the colony. Other mulattoes were free but poor, and still others were slaves.

HAITI *Land of Inequality*

> *[French laws] divided the offspring of white[s] and black[s] . . . into 128 divisions. The true Mulatto was the child of the pure black and the pure white.*

There were differences in status among the blacks, or noirs, too. Most remained slaves, but some had been freed, and many of those had escaped into the mountains. Escaped slaves, or Maroons, fought the French in **guerrilla** battles throughout most of the eighteenth century. In 1786 the French government officially granted the Maroons their freedom and a territory of their own.

Deep social, economic, and racial divisions among the early inhabitants characterized colonial life in Saint Domingue. So attuned was colonial culture to social division and especially to racial division that French laws governing the colony recognized 128 different racial classifications. This persistent attention to differences among people and the social and economic inequities that resulted meant that the colony was a breeding ground of resentment and violence.

REVOLUTIONARY TIMES

As the number and status of mulattoes in Saint Domingue increased during the eighteenth century, the colonial government grew nervous, and the poor whites became increasingly resentful. There was fear that mulattoes would soon outnumber whites. Colonial law granted to free mulattoes the same rights that whites enjoyed, so it appeared that mulattoes could eventually dominate Saint Domingue. To preserve the privileged social status of whites, therefore, the French gradually took away the rights that earlier had been granted to free mulattoes and to free blacks. Even the

A mulatto woman—from a class of free settlers of mixed ethnic background—meets with two slaves. Great resentment had built up among the classes in early Saint Domingue.

wealthiest mulattoes became subject to repression.

By 1781 it was illegal for whites to marry mulattoes. Mulattoes could not carry firearms. No mulatto could be addressed with respect as "Monsieur" or "Madame." They were segregated into special sections of theaters and churches and were forbidden to wear fashionable clothing or to ride in carriages. Any white man could insult or abuse a mulatto without fear of penalty, and mulattoes always lost in court. Any gens de couleur who raised a hand against a white could be sentenced to have that arm cut off.

In 1789 the revolutionary National Assembly in Paris, France, proclaimed that all men have free and equal rights. The mulattoes of Saint Domingue hoped that the proclamation applied to them just as it did to other French subjects. They hoped the outcome of the French Revolution (1789–1799) would restore to them their rights. This hope was strengthened when a mulatto petition of rights was brought before the National Assembly in October 1789.

To the mulatto leader, Vincent Ogé, the time seemed right to demand that the French colonial government in Saint Domingue restore the rights of mulattoes according to justice and

In July 1789, Paris mobs stormed a prison known as the Bastille. This event sparked the French Revolution. During the revolution, the battle between the French nobles and the common people represented a fight for social equality. In addition, many French urged the abolition of slavery in French colonies. These ideals spread to Saint Domingue, where a movement to end slavery took shape.

Library of Congress (LC-USZ62-1088)

HAITI *Land of Inequality*

Bearing the flag of the French Revolution, Vincent Ogé returned to Saint Domingue from France with news of the French decree giving mulattoes equal rights with whites. But the island's whites refused to acknowledge the decree, inciting a rebellion. Although Ogé's mulatto rebellion failed, it laid the groundwork for future uprisings in the colony.

© Roger-Viollet

the laws of France. Colonial leaders would not agree to this. They feared that by recognizing the rights of mulattoes, they would eventually have to recognize the rights of black slaves. This, in turn, would lead to the end of slavery and would jeopardize the prosperity of the plantation system.

Late in 1790, Ogé led an uprising of mulattoes in northern Saint Domingue. But most gens de couleur in Saint Domingue were unaware of Ogé and his plans, so the mulatto rebel led a force of only about 300. Knowing that mulatto supremacy depended on the subjugation of blacks, Ogé did not ask the slaves to join his cause. The mulattoes (many of whom were slaveholders) were fighting only for their own interests. Greatly outnumbered by white soldiers, Ogé and his men were captured, and Ogé was tortured and killed.

Ogé's execution caused an outcry in France. Moved to action, the National Assembly issued a decree on May 15, 1791, confirming the right of free, landowning, male gens de couleur (whose parents were both free) to vote and

The slaves of Saint Domingue had had enough. Meeting under the pretense of a voodoo ceremony, a rebel leader named Boukman orchestrated the event with several slave leaders. The rebellion on the French was swift and cruel.

to hold elected office. Although the decree affected only 400 people, white colonists were outraged, and the persecution of gens de couleur increased.

Meanwhile, the slaves of northern Saint Domingue were plotting a rebellion of their own. Under cover of voodoo services, slave representatives from several plantations met at night to organize their revolt. Their leader was a voodoo priest named Boukman.

REBELLION YEARS

On the night of August 14, 1791, Boukman held a ceremony in the woods of Bois Caïman. The assembled slaves swore an oath of obedience to the leaders of the revolt and swore death to all foreigners, or *blan.*

On the night of August 22, drumbeats throughout the north signaled the slaves to attack. By the tens of thousands, armed with pruning hooks, machetes, and torches, the slaves rose up against their owners. Embittered by the cruelty they and their families had endured in slavery, the slaves took revenge, burning hundreds of plantations and slaughtering French men, women, and children. The revolt spread and, by the end of August, half of the northern plain was in flames.

It is estimated that, during the weeks of fighting, more than 10,000 slaves and 2,000 French were killed. Many whites who were not killed fled to France. More than 1,000 plantations were sacked and burned. The pattern of violence begetting violence was firmly established.

At first the rebellion was confined to the north, and the only mulattoes to join the revolt against the French were in the northeast. But in September 1791, when the National Assembly revoked its May 15 decree giving political rights to gens de couleur, outraged mulattoes attacked the French in the south and west.

By 1792 all of Saint Domingue was involved in the fighting. Yet the various factions that might have formed alliances could rarely agree on a common interest. Instead, this period was characterized by shifting allegiances, by frequent betrayals, and by extreme brutality, torture, and vengeance on all sides.

To restore order to Saint Domingue, France sent 6,000 soldiers and three new commissioners to the colony. Once order returned, the commissioners had instructions to enforce another decree from the National Assembly, this time granting full and equal rights to all gens de couleur and all free blacks. Upon hearing the decree, outraged whites broke the peace, and the French commissioners were forced to become involved in the racial conflict. The commis-

Former slave François-Dominique Toussaint-Louverture had his first taste of freedom during the slave uprising. A French priest had illegally taught him to read and write, and books on the abolition of slavery inspired the young Haitian.

© Schomburg Center/Astor, Lenox, and Tilden Foundations

sioners, led by Léger-Félicité Sonthonax, called on noirs to help defend themselves against armed and angry whites who refused to obey the Paris decree. Thousands of slaves descended from the hills, driving most of the remaining whites out of Saint Domingue. On August 29, 1793, without authorization from Paris, Sonthonax declared the slaves free. Only later did he tell the National Assembly what he had done.

TOUSSAINT-LOUVERTURE

On the same day that Sonthonax declared the slaves free, François-Dominique Toussaint-Louverture issued a proclamation declaring his devotion to establishing liberty and equality in Saint Domingue and inviting his fellow islanders to join him.

An educated former slave, Toussaint joined the slave revolt when he was 45 years old and quickly rose to become the aide of the noir

Complicated Alliances

In 1792 the alliances in Saint Domingue were so complicated that at least five different, but simultaneous, factional configurations can be identified:
1. Slaves, under noir leadership, vs. French colonists
2. Slaves and mulattoes vs. French colonists
3. Slaves vs. French colonists and mulattoes
4. Slave-owning mulattoes vs. colonists
5. Colonists and their slaves vs. mulattoes

leaders. By 1793 he was the leader of his own force of 600 noirs. As a result, when Spain and Britain tried to take advantage of French weakness and to divide Saint Domingue between them, Toussaint was well positioned to use the opportunity to increase his own power and influence by playing off the feuding European powers.

In February 1793, Toussaint declared his allegiance to Spain. Placed in charge of 4,000 noir soldiers and receiving orders directly from the Spaniards, Toussaint quickly helped Spain conquer most of northern and central Saint Domingue. The British, meanwhile, took control of much of the west.

The French were on the brink of losing all of Saint Domingue. The mulatto leaders in the far north and in the south, who had allied themselves with France, were equally desperate. As soon as France ratified the abolition of slavery in February 1794, Toussaint, who had been secretly communicating with the French colonial governor, betrayed his Spanish allies.

Fighting against the other noir leaders who remained

Toussaint (above) *impressed two leaders of the rebellion with his knowledge of European military tactics, and they asked his advice. His understanding of battle maneuvers helped put the rebel army on equal footing with the European troops.*

© Schomburg Center

loyal to Spain, Toussaint quickly restored control of much of Saint Domingue to France. He did not strive to restore French rule, however. Once he had consolidated his power in Saint Domingue, Toussaint began once again to work against the weakened French forces. From 1795 to 1799, he used his expertise to outsmart and outmaneuver the French leaders, eventually driving them back to France. Toussaint remained the most powerful man in Saint Domingue.

CIVIL WAR

Toussaint was not alone in his efforts to overthrow the French colonial power in Saint Domingue. In the south, the mulatto leader, André Rigaud, had also outmaneuvered the French and was in complete control there. In his southern domain, gens de couleur ruled, and the noirs were re-enslaved.

Throughout the rebellion years, the French played mulatto interests against noir interests to maintain control and, later, to weaken both Toussaint and Rigaud. The last French commissioner to leave Saint Domingue made one final attempt to disrupt

When the islanders weren't combating European forces, they were fighting one another. Jean-Jaques Dessalines (left) joined Toussaint's noir forces in battling the mulattoes in the War of Knives. The mulatto troops, led by, among others, Jean-Pierre Boyer (center) and Alexandre Pétion (right), were soundly defeated. But the noir victory would not last long.

power by promoting Rigaud to equal military rank with Toussaint. He declared Rigaud the independent commander of the south, which gave him power to act independently of Toussaint. With this action, the French commissioner explicitly set noirs against mulattoes.

The first predictable consequence of this action was the almost immediate outbreak of civil war. As Rigaud led his troops against Toussaint, mulattoes in areas under noir control rose up to join Rigaud. They followed Alexandre Pétion and Jean-Pierre Boyer, mulatto officers who had once been loyal to Toussaint.

Toussaint's response was fierce and merciless. In what became known as the War of Knives, the noir leader used his superior numbers to overpower the mulatto opposition. With the help of his allies Henri Christophe and Jean-Jacques Dessalines, Toussaint emerged victorious. Rigaud, Pétion, Boyer, and the other senior mulatto officers escaped into exile.

Toussaint appointed Dessalines governor of the south. Dessalines's instructions were to purge the south of Rigaud loyalists. It is estimated that Dessalines's troops tortured and killed between 5,000 and 10,000 gens de couleur.

The civil war and the ensuing bloodbath seriously compromised the ability of noirs and mulattoes to work together to build a new nation. The battles and betrayals of the 1790s would not be forgotten.

TOUSSAINT'S GOVERNMENT

Although Saint Domingue was not yet formally an independent nation, Toussaint began establishing a new system of government. In 1801 his handpicked assembly presented the first constitution. Toussaint was declared governor-general for life and had the authority to choose his successor. All power was centralized, and Toussaint had the capacity to make and enforce all laws, appoint all government officials, control finances, and command the armies. He set up the fledgling nation as a military dictatorship.

His new government was also corrupt. High-ranking government officials used state finances to enrich themselves. Dessalines, for example, owned 33 plantations by 1801. Parts of the budget were diverted into secret and private accounts. The courts acted arbitrarily and were influenced by bribery.

Toussaint ruled over a land that a decade of fighting had completely destroyed. The agricultural economy that produced the island's wealth and that alone could provide the money Toussaint needed to maintain and arm his troops, needed to be rebuilt as quickly as possible. Yet the most profitable crops were

> *By tying the noirs to the land and making them subject to military control, Toussaint established an oppressive relationship between the peasantry . . . and the state.*

labor intensive, and the former slaves were not eager to return to plantation life.

Toussaint believed he had to find a way to put people back to work without reinstituting slavery. His solution was a system called **fermage,** created by Henri Christophe. Under fermage, the government took over abandoned farmland and rented it to army officers or other public officials. Former slaves were then assigned to the new plantations with orders to work the land according to fixed hours and established working conditions. The laborers received food, shelter, and one quarter of the crop revenue, with the remainder divided between the tenant and the government.

The former slaves worked under military supervision and were not allowed to leave their plantations. Army generals roamed the countryside, inspecting the plantations and making sure

everybody worked. Those who slacked off were beaten. Anyone who refused to work could be executed. Although working conditions had improved since colonial days, the former slaves were in the service of the state instead of private landholders.

Although dependent on forced labor, economic productivity improved markedly under the system of fermage. But by tying the noirs to the land and making them subject to military control, Toussaint established an oppressive relationship between the peasantry (a class of poor, rural subsistence farmers) and the state. In addition, military soldiers who enforced the rules of the state were given special privileges, no matter what their skin color.

Despite these problems, Toussaint's government provided administrative organization to the island. It stabilized the currency, suppressed smuggling, opened new schools, and built roads. There was some hope that the island could resume its place as an important trading partner with other nations.

The new government and its system of fermage did not meet with universal approval. On October 22, 1801, laborers in the north rose up in rebellion. Toussaint and his generals were quick to crush the insurrection. Dessalines and his troops executed the revolt's leaders and, according to one estimate, killed a quarter of the laborers in the rebel districts.

FIGHT FOR INDEPENDENCE

Toussaint undisputedly ruled Saint Domingue, but he had never officially declared the country's independence from France. In 1802, when Napoleon of France signed a peace agreement with Britain that ended years of war between them, Napoleon felt France would have the time and the resources to regain control of Saint Domingue.

To that end, Napoleon sent his brother-in-law, Charles-Victor-Emmanuel Leclerc, to Saint

Napoleon sent Charles-Victor-Emmanuel Leclerc (right) to Saint Domingue with secret instructions to defeat the rebels and to restore slavery. The plan was that Leclerc was to first win over the rebel leaders with false promises to gain their confidence and then to defeat their troops. But the rebel leaders, suspicious of the French, did not fall for the plot.

© Roger-Viollet

Not trusting the French, Toussaint had prepared his men for the worst. He had stockpiled arms in the mountains and had stationed his troops along the coasts and in the cities. The French ships landed in Le Cap on February 2, 1802. Two days later, the city was in flames.

Domingue at the head of some 21,000 troops. Leclerc's secret instructions were to win over the black leaders, send them to France, disarm the noir army, smash any organized resistance, and restore slavery. Leclerc reached the island in February 1802. With him were Rigaud, Pétion, Boyer, and other mulatto officers exiled to France after the War of Knives.

Toussaint knew the French were coming, and he did not trust them. But he also knew that, with inferior arms and fewer soldiers, he could not defeat them in open combat. He adopted a scorched-earth policy, choosing to destroy the island rather than to give in. He gave instructions to burn the towns, to lay waste to the countryside, to kill any whites on the island, and to retreat to the hills.

Within weeks the noir defenders had blown up or burned much of Saint Domingue, killing any white civilians they encountered. But by April 1802, it was clear that the French were not succumbing to tropical diseases as Toussaint had hoped. French forces remained strong, and Toussaint's defenses were crumbling. In May Toussaint negotiated a surrender and was given safe

> *[Toussaint] adopted a scorched-earth policy, choosing to destroy the island rather than to give in [to the French].*

passage to retire to his plantation. In June, however, Leclerc tricked Toussaint into attending a private meeting, arrested him, brought him secretly to a waiting ship, and sent him to prison in France. Toussaint died less than a year later.

Tropical diseases did eventually take their toll on the French forces. When Leclerc succumbed to yellow fever (a tropical virus transmitted by mosquitoes) in October 1802, General Rochambeau succeeded him. Rochambeau was notoriously cruel and politically inept. Leclerc had covertly implemented Napoleon's decrees to strip gens de couleur of equal rights and to reinstitute slavery of the noirs.

Ten officers awaited Toussaint at the French headquarters. When he arrived, Toussaint realized he was outnumbered and surrendered (left). He and his whole family were sent to France, where Toussaint was imprisoned. General Rochambeau (above) openly rejected France's decree to give mulattoes equal rights, unintentionally giving Saint Domingue's divided factions a reason to combine forces.

Rochambeau, on the other hand, outwardly executed the decrees. However, he unintentionally succeeded in creating a common cause to unite the noirs and the mulattoes—an unprecedented alliance in the racially split colony.

Under the leadership of Pétion, a Rigaud supporter, the mulattoes joined Dessalines and his noir forces in fighting to expel the French. By the end of 1803, the French were defeated. Dessalines, who had led the joint forces, declared independence on January 1, 1804, reclaiming its former Arawak Indian name of Haiti. The new nation was the first independent black state in the Western Hemisphere.

Yet the bloodshed was not over. In declaring independence, the Haitians swore to kill all French colonists in Haiti. The massacre of several thousand French colonists began in February, and by April almost every French man, woman, and child on the island had been killed.

According to Haiti's first constitution, ratified in May 1805, all Haitians were to be known henceforward as noirs.

In a final fight for freedom, the noir army defeated French troops in 1803.

Bibliothèque Nationale

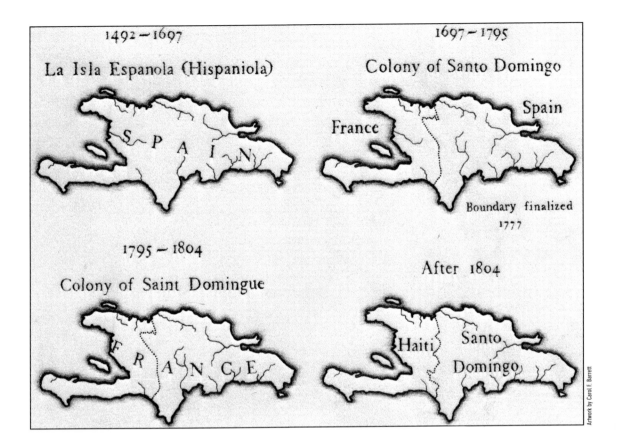

1492 – 1697

La Isla Española (Hispaniola)

S P A I N

1697 – 1795

Colony of Santo Domingo

France

Spain

Boundary finalized
1777

1795 – 1804

Colony of Saint Domingue

F R A N C E

After 1804

Haiti

Santo
Domingo

Artwork by Carol F. Barrett

No foreigners, moreover, could own property in Haiti. And should the French return, the constitution provided that the towns would be destroyed and the nation would rise in arms. Finally, the constitution granted all governing power to Dessalines, who crowned himself emperor. In the tradition established by Toussaint, Haiti was to be a military dictatorship.

A NATION STILL DIVIDED

In killing the remaining French civilians, Dessalines guaranteed that an outraged France would not recognize the new nation of Haiti. The first free, black nation in the Western Hemisphere found itself isolated, poor, and surrounded by hostile, slave-owning powers.

Although they had fought with mulattoes against the French, Dessalines and many

Control of the island of Hispaniola changed hands several times between the French and the Spanish before Haiti declared its independence from the colonial powers. Nearly 300 years of European occupation had left their mark, giving each of the two territories its own language, religion, and set of class divisions.

other noirs distrusted gens de couleur. Mulattoes were descendants of the hated French colonists and had owned slaves. For their part, the mulattoes knew Dessalines's violent, suspicious nature and remembered the bloodbath following the War of Knives.

In addition to the divisions between noirs and mulattoes, the entire population of Haiti was divided between the military (about 15 percent of the population) and agricultural laborers, known as cultivators. As in Toussaint's government, cultivators were forced to work the land under military supervision. Although the slave master's whip was outlawed, there was no shortage of permissible alternative tools with which to beat the laborers.

In addition, the country was divided between the corrupt court of Emperor Dessalines and the general populace. Public funds were used for private gain, while the pressing needs of the Haitian economy and the Haitian poor were ignored.

A revolt against Dessalines's regime was not long in coming. It began in the mulatto-dominated south. When the emperor heard of the up-

Henri Christophe, ruler of northern Haiti, was among the first leaders of the newly independent Haiti.

risings in mid-October 1806, he immediately marched south to suppress the revolt. But on the way to Port-au-Prince, Dessalines's advance guard decided to join the revolt. Together with rebel leader Pétion, the advance guard planned an ambush. Emperor Dessalines was hacked to death with the help of his own men.

The assassination of Dessalines resulted in the political division of Haiti. In the north, Henri Christophe was

Citadelle Laferrière, a fortress built during Christophe's rule, still stands as a reminder of his regime.

© Schomburg Center

proclaimed president of the State of Haiti in 1807. In the south, Alexandre Pétion was elected president of the Republic of Haiti. Another civil war quickly developed. After six more years of fighting, both between and among mulatto and noir factions, Haiti remained politically split. Christophe ruled a noir kingdom in northern Haiti, and Pétion ruled a mulatto republic in the south and west. ⊕

3

ENTRENCHED POSITIONS

Christophe crowned himself King Henri I in 1811. His rule was characterized by military rigor and absolute incorruptibility. It was also marked by a striking increase in prosperity. He established what was called the Code Rural to help organize life in the kingdom. The Code Rural, a more elaborate version of fermage, was efficient but severe. Noir farmers were bound to the land. They worked Monday through Friday, beginning at 3:00 A.M. with mandatory prayers and breakfast and ending at sundown. On Saturday the farmers could cultivate their own gardens and go to the market, and Sunday was a day of rest. In return for their labor, the cultivators were clothed, fed, and paid one quarter of the total yield. The law was en-

When Christophe declared himself king of northern Haiti, he established a new capital at Cap-Haïtien. There workers built the impressive San Souci Palace as Christophe's private home.

Library of Congress (LC-USZ62-99749)

forced by King Henri's royal guard, which also governed the kingdom's 56 localities in northern Haiti.

With the steady income this system produced, King Henri administered the kingdom and built numerous palaces and forts. He committed himself to creating an elite class of educated noir. He established five schools with the help of a series of British schoolmasters. Those children who skipped school were locked up for a week with nothing to eat but bread and water.

Alexandre Pétion, by contrast, presided during an era of economic decline in southern Haiti. Rather than trying to force his people to work in a plantation economy, Pétion redistributed the land in increasingly smaller plots. These plots, however, were too small to sustain the large-scale production that was needed to make export crops profitable. No longer able to produce cash crops (except for coffee, which grew wild on the hillsides), farmers produced only what they needed to feed themselves. The southern republic became a nation of subsistence farmers.

Pétion died in 1818 without naming a successor. The mulatto officer Jean-Pierre Boyer eventually was declared the new president for life. Less than 18 months later, King Henri suffered a stroke. His soldiers and generals, long resentful of their king's strict discipline, immediately conspired to take advantage of his weakness. Rather than face their wrath, King Henri shot himself in the heart. Within two weeks, Boyer had marched north at the head of 20,000 men. In 1820 Haiti was reunited. Not incidentally, the multi-million-dollar surplus in King Henri's royal treasury fell under Boyer's control. A year later, Boyer took advantage of neighboring Santo Domingo's revolt against the Spaniards and conquered the eastern end of the island.

DEBT AND DECAY

In three years, Boyer had spent the entire surplus in King Henri's treasury, and the north as well as the south were impoverished. In 1824 the government spent more than it took in.

Haiti slowly slid into ruin. Buildings, both in the towns and in the countryside, collapsed from neglect. Once-productive fields grew wild. Bridges collapsed, and the few roads that countless battles had destroyed were never repaired. Politicians diverted tax money earmarked for rebuilding the nation's infrastructure into their own pockets.

In addition, Haiti was isolated both economically and diplomatically. No foreign government recognized the new black nation. Slave-holding countries, including the United States, feared that the idea of black freedom and equality would threaten the status quo in their own nations.

Other countries also withheld recognition for fear of offending France, which still claimed Haiti and would not overlook the slaughter of French citizens in 1804. Recognition by the French, therefore, seemed a necessary first step if Haiti were ever to participate as an equal partner in international relations and trade.

But French recognition of Haiti came at a price. In 1825 King Charles X of France decreed that France would grant Haitians independence after Haiti paid France compensation for French losses. The price was 150 million francs. Independence was conditional until Haiti paid the full indemnity over a five-year period.

The terms set by France were humiliating and impossible to meet since Haiti was virtually bankrupt. Many asked why free citizens of Haiti should owe anything to their former slaveholders and plantation owners. The noir masses felt that Boyer and his fellow mulattoes, in seeking recognition from France, had betrayed them yet again.

1826 CODE RURAL

To resurrect the Haitian economy and to raise funds to pay the French indemnity, Boyer legislated another version of fermage known as the 1826 Code Rural. The code stated that all Haitians, except the army and the elite ("elite" was understood to mean mulattoes), were cultivators. Cultivators, as before, were tied to the land and were forced to work it. The army and a large body of **bureaucrats** enforced and managed the system. Bureaucrats collected and distributed all proceeds.

By exempting the mulattoes from the subservient role of cultivator, the 1826 Code Rural legalized the division of the country into a mulatto elite, which controlled the government and commerce, and poor noirs, who could not leave their small plots of land. Boyer further protected the status of mulattoes by denying education to the noirs. For black Haitians, the only route off the land and to improved social and economic status was to serve in the army.

Boyer's code granted the army officials control of the Haitian population except within Port-au-Prince. Army officers had complete authority, including the ability to condemn rural people to death. There were no restrictions to keep army officers from robbing peasants at will.

The huge and inefficient bureaucracy Boyer established to manage this system channeled money to the mulatto elite. Boyer created more than enough positions in the bureaucracy for every literate mulatto male in the country, and each one was paid from the proceeds created by the Code Rural. This bureaucracy presented irresistible opportunities for corruption.

Because of inefficiency and corruption, the 1826 Code Rural did not improve Haitian economic productivity. In fact, the system could not have succeeded because it was based on large-scale production by a disciplined agricultural sector, whereas Haiti was mostly a land of small-scale subsistence farmers.

In 1838 the French recognized that Haiti was unable to pay the indemnity. France renegotiated the terms, giving Haiti unconditional independence and reducing the indemnity to 60 million francs, to be paid over 30 years. This was still far more than Haiti could afford.

SUCCESSIVE REVOLTS

A restless army overthrew Boyer in 1844, and Santo Domingo declared independence from Boyer's successor. From 1844 to 1915, Haiti had 22 different heads of state as the country was torn by a series of revolts, secessions, and reunifications. The countryside became poorer and poorer. Landowners moved to the cities, further dividing the population into urban elite and rural poor.

Throughout this period, most of Haiti's presidents

Faustin-Élie Soulouque's time in power (1847–1859) resembled the regimes of other Haitian rulers. From 1813 to 1915, 16 out of 22 Haitian rulers were overthrown. Only 1 served a full term in office. During those same years, Haiti suffered through at least 102 armed insurrections.

were black military leaders. Real political power, however, usually lay with the mulatto elite, which pulled the strings of the black puppet leaders. The black military enjoyed the privileges of the mulatto elite by suppressing the noir farmers and endorsing mulatto supremacy. But when noir leaders gained true control, their resentment of mulatto power combined explosively with the mulatto refusal to be governed by a noir.

Here is one incident. Mulatto ministers appointed noir general, Faustin-Élie Soulouque, president in 1847. Born a slave, Soulouque initially allowed the ministers to exercise authority through him. But, confident of his support in the army, Soulouque soon assumed full command. When a prominent mulatto politician was found in a house full of weapons, Soulouque armed the rural people and told them to await his signal. A week later, leading men in Port-au-Prince, mostly mulatto politicians and merchants along with some noirs, were lured into the palace yard, where the presidential guard fired at them. On signal, the armed farmers surged into town, looting and destroying mulatto stores and homes. Soulouque's firing squads spent days systematically eliminating his mulatto opposition.

In another instance, a noir leader named Louis-Étienne-Félicité Salomon assumed the presidency in 1879. He found his attempts to institute meaningful economic and social reforms challenged by the mulatto opposition.

© Jean Loup Charmet

Salomon became frustrated by repeated failed attempts at revolution and by a steady refusal of the opposition to answer his pleas for cooperation. On Saturday, September 22, 1883, Salomon's troops armed noir volunteers at the National Palace. All day long, soldiers and volunteers rampaged through the mulatto business district, burning, looting, and killing. The next day, farmers rioted throughout the elite neighborhoods. In the ensuing massacre, which became known as La Semaine Sanglante (Bloody Week), it is estimated that noirs killed as many as 4,000 mulattoes.

Amid the economic conflict and social antagonism that fueled the fight for power, peasant-based militias surfaced to cash in on Haiti's political upheaval. For example, an aspiring politician could hire a peasant army of *cacos*, or "kingmakers," to overthrow the ruling president and install their employer in exchange for a large sum of money and looting rights during their offensive. A series of Cacos Revolts, as they were known, flared up between 1867 and 1920. These revolts represented not

The crushing debt that resulted from the payment of the French indemnity was the cause of many of Haiti's future troubles. Debt became the excuse for repeated foreign interventions in Haiti, and it was the means by which foreigners gained control of Haiti's finances. Much of Haiti's extreme poverty can be attributed indirectly, if not always directly, to the payment of the indemnity.

racial tensions between noirs and mulattoes, but a violent response from the farmers, who wanted land and better economic conditions.

Throughout the turmoil of nineteenth-century Haiti, the needs of the people and of the nation as a whole were largely overlooked. Noir factions, dominated by the military, were generally dedicated to maintaining the absolute power of individual leaders, while mulatto parties tended to support mulatto group interests exclusively. Rather than leading to economic and social reforms that improved the lives of most Haitians, the political conflicts ultimately led to increased repression of the general populace. Since the more moderate regimes suffered the majority of insurrections, Haiti's most ruthless leaders claimed that their harshness was necessary to maintain order.

FROM CRISIS THROUGH OCCUPATION

Without a productive economy, successive governments had to be creative about generating revenue. The main sources of money were foreign loans and export and import taxes. By 1891 export and import taxes made up 98 percent of government revenue.

Distribution of these taxes further widened the gulf between rich and poor. High export taxes on coffee provided 60 to 90 percent of government revenues from the late 1800s through the 1950s. To sell their coffee in the international market, small-scale farmers had to price it at low cost to accommodate the additional export tax. This effectively reduced agricultural income, earned by a majority of Haitians, by 40 percent. The government heavily taxed imported necessities, such as flour, oil, candles, kerosene, matches, and food. By contrast, it did not tax imported luxuries such as opera glasses and automobiles as much.

Foreign immigrants, especially French, German, U.S., Italian, Syrian, Lebanese, and English merchants, dominated the import-export businesses. Their governments, in turn, began to dominate the Haitian economy. Foreign gunboats repeatedly took up threatening positions offshore to reinforce economic claims, to protect the lives and interests of their citizens in Haiti, or to gain political concessions from the Haitian government.

By the early 1900s, 80 percent of Haitian government revenues went to pay foreign debts and indemnities, leaving only 20 percent for education, for support of the military, and for other government functions. And although millions of dollars passed through government hands, Haiti had little to show

for it. Those with power used it only to enrich themselves.

These economic problems threatened Haiti's sovereignty. In 1914 the United States watched as internal struggles for government control in Haiti seemed to threaten the Haitian National Bank (then owned by German, French, and U.S. investors). Concerned about the security of the bank, about German influence in Haiti as World War I (1914–1918) approached, and about the security of the

nearby Panama Canal, the United States acted to protect its own interests. In December 1914, U.S. marines landed in Haiti and seized all the gold from the Haitian National Bank. The marines sent it back to New York for safekeeping.

In July 1915, Haitian president Vilbrun Guillaume Sam was overthrown and killed. Concluding that no legitimate authority was left in Haiti, the United States orchestrated a military takeover of the country.

U.S. marines landed in Haiti in July 1915. The United States declared that it was acting to prevent possible anarchy and was responding to President Sam's overthrow. But U.S. warships had been patrolling Haitian waters as early as July 1914 during customs negotiations.

Although the occupying forces oversaw the election of a new Haitian president, the United States dictated every decision he made.

The U.S. occupation of Haiti lasted from 1915 to 1934. During that time, the U.S. occupying forces dissolved the Haitian army and replaced it with a U.S.-trained and U.S.-led police force. The United States also took control of the Haitian

> *Roped together like slaves, underfed and brutally overworked, the corvée laborers worked under overseers who gunned down any man who attempted escape.*

National Bank and the customhouses (buildings where customs, or duty taxes, are collected and vessels receive clearance), giving the United States effective control of all public finance. In 1918 the United States imposed a new constitution that allowed foreign nationals to own property in Haiti. As a result, multinational compa-

Three lieutenants of the U.S.-led army, called the Gendarmerie d'Haïti, pose with Haitian president Philippe Sudre Dartiguenave. The United States's fourth choice for president, the former senator had agreed to support several policies that favored the United States before becoming president in August 1915.

The gendarmerie (above), *predecessor of the modern-day Haitian military, patrolled the countryside. Unlike the pre-occupation army, which defended its territory, the new army fought Haitian citizens to gain command for an elite few.*

The U.S. army used force and bribery to weaken various anti-U.S. factions. To suppress resistance, U.S. officials circulated photographs of assassinated rebel leader Charlemagne Peralte (above). Haitians, instead, saw him as a martyr for Haitian liberty.

nies began buying up the most fertile land in Haiti.

The United States occupied the Dominican Republic and Haiti simultaneously. During the occupation, Haiti's economy and infrastructure improved. Before the takeover, only a few miles of roadway were paved. By the end of the occupation, workers had built more than 1,000 miles of all-weather roads and 210 major bridges. Airports, lighthouses, and telephone and telegraph systems were also in place.

The occupying forces modernized Haiti's infrastructure by reviving the old system of forced labor. Rural residents feared that the corvée, as the system was called, was the beginning of a return to slavery. Many Haitians also believed that the U.S. occupiers favored the mulatto elite, which were appointed to most positions of power.

Yet neither noir nor mulatto Haitians welcomed the military rule of foreigners. Large-scale guerrilla warfare, long a feature of Haitian political life, turned against the occupying forces. The urban mulatto elite secretly lent support and encouragement to those fighting the U.S. forces and openly waged a propaganda campaign to discredit the United States. Although U.S. troops suppressed the armed resistance to the occupation in 1920, the propaganda battles continued.

Many Haitians responded unfavorably to the U.S. occupation and took to the streets in protest. Their list of grievances was long, and the United States eventually withdrew its troops.

In 1929 the growing unpopularity of the U.S.-installed government in Haiti led to riots and strikes. Increased violence in Haiti as well as doubts within the United States about U.S. military policy led the United States to withdraw from Haiti in 1934, two years earlier than expected. The United States left behind a legacy of anti-American feeling and a mulatto elite that had consolidated its hold on economic and political power. It also left behind a well-trained military force as the most stable institution in Haiti.

THE FIRST DUVALIER

From 1934 to 1946, the mulatto elite remained in power. But the U.S. occupation, which had favored mulattoes, had provided a focus for black nationalism. Slowly Haiti's noirs came together in an organized movement to claim political power and to protect Afro-Haitian culture, Creole language, and voodoo traditions. In 1946 the military threw out the mulatto president, Élie Lescot. Under the military's supervision, the Haitian National Assembly elected a noir,

Paul Magloire (pictured with his family), *graduate of one of the first classes of the U.S.-run Military School, became Haiti's president in 1950.*

UPI/Corbis-Bettmann

Dumarsais Estimé, to the Haitian presidency.

In 1950 Estimé tried to change the constitution to lengthen his term of office. This time, however, the politically independent military intervened. Estimé was overthrown, and Paul Magloire, a colonel in the Haitian army, was installed. Magloire, in turn, was overthrown in 1956, as were a series of succeeding administrations.

In September 1957, François Duvalier was elected president. Duvalier, a noir, had grown up in a poor household, but he managed to change his economic status by hard work and study. Duvalier became a rural doctor and directed Haiti's programs to eradicate the tropical diseases yaws and malaria. His contributions to Haiti's public health programs earned him the nickname "Papa Doc."

Politically, Duvalier had been part of the 1946 black-power revolution. Duvalier was also a griot, a member of a society that preserves stories and religious traditions from Africa. He appeared to be the ideal representative of the hopes and aspirations of Haiti's black rural majority.

Military support was essential to Duvalier's election victory. The military shut down all political debate, forced other candidates

On September 22, 1957, [oppostion] supporter Marcell Hakime Bellande voted for François Duvalier. She did so because at nine in the morning armed Duvalierists broke into her house and forced her to accompany them to the polls.

François Duvalier (left, holding papers) *had substantial public support because of his* noiriste *(Afro-Haitian) platform. But his candidacy and election were backed by the military* (below), *which ultimately enabled him to win.*

out of the race, removed all members of the Supreme Court, and made it a crime to criticize or ridicule government and military officials. Voting fraud was widespread on election day.

Duvalier recognized that if the military could help bring him to power, it could also help remove him from office. He was determined to dismantle the military to consolidate power in his own hands. Through a series of transfers and forced retirements, Duvalier eliminated the top military leadership. The lower echelon officers, whom he promoted to high positions, owed him their total loyalty. The Military School, which previously had served as a training ground for future leaders was closed.

Instead of relying on the military and the police, Duvalier created the National Security Volunteers, better known as the Tontons Macoutes. Like the military and paramilitary groups that had terrorized Haiti in the 1800s, the Tontons Macoutes roamed the countryside as armed informants with free license from the government to harass the citizenry. No crime they committed was punished. No cruelty or brutality, including murder, was forbidden. Most Tontons Macoutes were noirs. Some came from rural backgrounds, others were non-mulatto traders from the towns, and others were criminals or former soldiers. The Tontons Macoutes adopted a recognizable uniform—dark glasses, jeans, a bandanna, a peasant hat, and a bulging gun holster—that contributed to the aura of fear that surrounded them. They lived by extorting money and food from the populace. They earned their privileges by absolute obedience to Duvalier.

Rural Haiti had long been governed by section chiefs, who worked for the government, collecting taxes and extorting money from peasants. Duvalier recruited these section chiefs into the Tontons Macoutes, whose demands were law. Crushed between fear of the section chiefs and an inability to grow enough food for their families, peasants fled to the cities, crowding the slums as they vainly looked for work.

Although the Tontons Macoutes were instrumental in enforcing Duvalier's rule, Duvalier also had support from the United States. He maintained this support by playing on U.S. fears of Communism, pointing to the just emerging Communist government of Fidel Castro in nearby Cuba. Duvalier made it clear that if the United States wanted Haiti

UPI/Corbis-Bettmann

Recruits for Duvalier's secret army, known as the Tontons Macoutes, learn to operate one of the six cannons surrounding the National Palace.

Whenever President Duvalier appeared in public, he was surrounded by armed soldiers and the Tontons Macoutes and was often armed himself.

to cooperate to stop the regional spread of Communism, the United States would have to assist Haiti by providing foreign aid.

Much of the U.S. aid to Haiti went directly into the pockets of Duvalier and his family. Even when foreign aid did result in improvements to Haiti's infrastructure, those improvements opened the countryside to increased exploitation by the urban elite and by foreign investors. This resulted in still more displacement of rural people and the increased migration of the poor into the cities.

In 1964, having consolidated his power, Duvalier changed the constitution and declared himself president for life. The Haitian government, meanwhile, became a tool to enrich the Duvalier family. The Duvalier regime imposed new taxes and payroll deductions, all of which

> *Socially [members of the Tontons] Macoutes came from the most disadvantaged classes and regarded the [National Security Volunteers] as their sole escape from the relentless misery and hard work that inevitably awaited them.*

were directed into Duvalier's personal bank accounts. Profits from state-controlled companies and employee contributions to a national pension fund were also major sources of the Haitian president's unofficial income.

In response to the terror and repression of the Duva-lier regime, many educated Haitians fled the country. Some went to the United States or Canada. Others left for Africa, where they served as teachers, doctors, and engineers. The crippling effects of the resulting "brain drain" were another blow to the Haitian economy.

Terror and poverty reigned in urban and rural areas alike during Papa Doc's dictatorship.

BABY DOC'S RULE

Papa Doc Duvalier died in 1971. He was succeeded in office by his 19-year-old son Jean-Claude Duvalier, known as "Baby Doc." Baby Doc also proclaimed himself president for life and imitated his father in the political uses of brute force and terror.

Baby Doc's regime, however, was not as repressive as his father's had been. It was characterized by periods of liberalization and reduced violence alternating with periods of renewed suppression and brutality. The violence would periodically let up as Baby Doc tried to adhere to the conditions that U.S. president Jimmy Carter had tied to foreign-aid dollars. Carter had called for human-rights improvements in Haiti. But these measures did not last long because Baby Doc feared that any policies of liberalization would develop a life of their own and would go farther than he had intended.

In 1980 Jean-Claude Duvalier married Michèle Bennett, a daughter of the mulatto elite. The wedding, which cost an estimated $7 million, signaled an alliance between the government and the mulatto business community and was seen by Haiti's noirs as a betrayal of

Guarded by the military his father had set up, Jean-Claude inherited the presidency, and the Duvalier legacy continued.

the few noiriste principles that Baby Doc's father had maintained. While Papa Doc's repressive regime had favored upwardly mobile black Haitians, Baby Doc became an agent for the advancement of mulatto interests.

Haiti's economic troubles deepened.

The people of Haiti had suffered through 30 years of Duvalierism. By the 1980s, they were starving. The exhausted Haitian soil produced less than half as much

time, the richest 1 percent of Haitians received 44 percent of the national income, owned 60 percent of the best land, and paid only 3.5 percent of the nation's taxes. The Haitian people had had enough. ⊕

Despite her notorious reputation for extravagance and cruelty, Michèle Bennett married Baby Doc on May 27, 1980. The union with a member of the mulatto elite cemented Baby Doc's ties with Haiti's powerful, mulatto community.

Michèle's well-publicized million-dollar shopping trips to Paris, her cocaine use, and her cruelty toward her mother-in-law (Papa Doc's widow) did not help her or her husband's public image. Resentment against the presidential couple increased as Michèle's mulatto family and friends joined in looting the public treasury, even as

rice per acre as in the Dominican Republic and less than one-fifth as much rice per acre as in the United States. Haiti was completely dependent on imported food to feed its population, but the people had no money to buy it. Prices for cooking oil tripled because Baby Doc's friends held a monopoly on the industry. At the same

4

THE PRESENT CONFLICT

In 1985, encouraged by a grassroots movement that originated within the Haitian Catholic churches, massive public demonstrations against the Duvalier regime erupted. The military, weakened under Papa Doc, had regained its strength and took the side of the protesters. Charging the Duvalier regime with human-rights abuses, the United States cut off foreign aid to Haiti and strongly encouraged the Duvaliers to leave the country. In the face of overwhelming internal and international pressure, Jean-Claude Duvalier and his family flew into exile in France on February 7, 1986.

Celebrating their freedom from dictatorship, millions of Haitians blew conch shells, sang, and danced in the streets. In the towns, people seized mansions and estates belonging to prominent Duvalier supporters. Rural Haitians threw out the corrupt section chiefs who had collected taxes for the Duvaliers and for themselves. Mobs attacked and drove away the Tontons Macoutes, taking violent revenge for decades of brutality.

UPI/Corbis-Bettmann

Scores of international journalists and photographers arrived to record the downfall of the Duvalier regime, as Baby Doc and Michèle fled to France (left). Facing page: Because of its proximity to U.S. shores and of its strategic location in the Caribbean Sea, Haiti has long had its affairs monitored and influenced by its large neighbor to the north.

Popular organizations that had opposed Duvalier—including church groups, farmers, labor unions, student movements, and neighborhood committees—organized to create a better future for their country. These organizations shared a commitment to the democratic participation of the people in their own government. Among their first priorities were campaigns to increase Haiti's literacy rate and to clean up Haiti's unsanitary slums.

Haitians hit the streets in celebration (above) *upon hearing the news of Baby Doc's departure. But many wanted revenge for the three decades of violence under the Duvalier dictatorships and lashed out at the Tontons Macoutes. Police officers dispersed angry Haitians* (right), *who were staking out the home of a Tonton Macoute.*

DUVALIERISM WITHOUT DUVALIER

The joy of the Haitian masses was short-lived, however. In a last-ditch attempt to secure power for his regime, Jean-Claude Duvalier had appointed members of the National Council of Government, headed by Lieutenant General Henri Namphy. In Port-au-Prince, the same officials who had governed under the Duvaliers remained in power under this military interim government, which quickly became known as "Duvalierism without Duvalier." The army and the Tontons Macoutes held the most significant power in the nation, and the economic elite continued to control the government and the wealth.

In 1986 the National Council of Government, dominated by Duvalierists and military leaders, organized the election of a legislative assembly. In a clear sign that most Haitians distrusted the election process, less than 5 percent of the people voted. Once in office,

Celebrations did not last long, as the military regrouped and installed Henri Namphy (in front), an army officer, as president.

Reuters/Corbis-Bettmann

Reaction to government-controlled elections was strong, as angry protesters violently aired their frustrations.

Reuters/Corbis-Bettmann

the assembly drafted a new constitution that banned top Duvalierists from political office, limited the powers of the president, removed military control of elections, and guaranteed many political freedoms to the people. It was approved by almost every political organization, as well as by the Catholic Church. Almost half the population voted in the referendum (a popular vote on matters proposed by the legislature) on the new constitution, and it was approved by 99.8 percent of those voting.

The new constitution called for elections in November 1987 to replace the members of the interim government. The civilian opposition to the interim government, including most popular organizations, agreed to participate in the election. Long before November, the political campaigning turned into a campaign of terror designed to assure the continued rule of the military leaders and Duvalierists.

Soldiers killed hundreds of farmers who had been

organizing for land reform in the rural town of Jean-Rabel. In Port-au-Prince the military responded to general strikes with attacks that killed dozens of protesters. During a Mass, soldiers attacked the church of Father Jean-Bertrand Aristide. Aristide had been vocal in opposing the Duvalier regime and was deeply involved in the popular political movement. Gunmen shot parishioners as they prayed, and assassins pursued Aristide. Presidential candidates were beaten and assassinated. In June the National Council of Government dissolved the country's biggest labor group, the Independent Haitian Workers' Organization. A week before the November election, Namphy named himself head of the armed forces for the next three years.

On election day, soldiers and Tontons Macoutes stole ballot boxes and beat people as they tried to vote. Sixteen people were killed as they stood in line to vote in a schoolyard in Port-au-Prince. Namphy used the violence as a pretext to cancel the voting less than three hours after it had begun. Leslie Manigat became the new army-elected president.

Ignoring international criticism and violently suppressing the growing dissent within Haiti, Namphy scheduled a second election for January 1988. He named his own electoral council to oversee the election, abolished voter registration and secret balloting, and required candidates to print and distribute their own ballots.

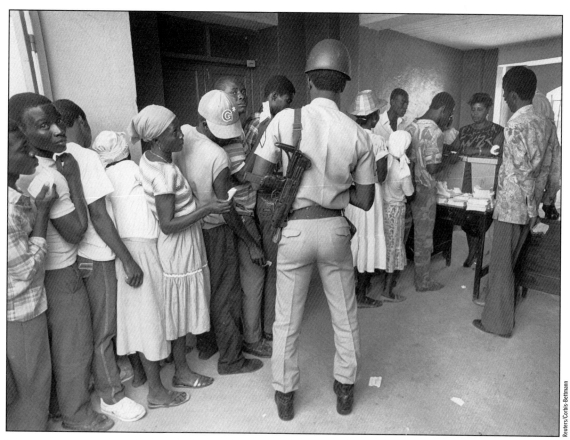

Voter turnout was low for the presidential election in January 1990. Armed soldiers guarded most polling stations.

The January elections were boycotted by all opposition groups and were denounced by the international community as unfair. Less than 10 percent of eligible voters cast their ballots. Many of those who voted, however, did so repeatedly. In the town of Saint Marc, northwest of Port-au-Prince, two truckloads of government workers cast ballots so often that 50 people accounted for nearly 800 votes. Manigat, a pro-military candidate with little political backing in Haiti, was again declared the presidential winner, and Namphy remained head of the armed forces. Less than six months later, Namphy deposed Manigat and took back the presidency.

In mid-September, however, another group of military officers, led by Lieutenant General Prosper Avril, threw out Namphy and took over the government. By then the Haitian economy was in complete collapse. Military leaders jockeyed for position, and Avril narrowly survived a coup attempt in April 1989. Less than a year later, he was forced to resign and sent into exile in the United States.

When the international community decided to step in and oversee elections in Haiti, Ertha Pascal-Trouillot, a Haitian Supreme Court justice, became provisional president of the country. She viewed her primary role as leading Haiti to a democratic government. Father Aristide saw his chance to affect change in Haiti but bided his time, knowing he would meet with opposition. Two months before the election, he announced his candidacy. Until then, Marc Bazin, the favored candidate of the United States, was expected to win, but Aristide's announcement had wide popular support.

The National Front for Change and Democracy, an alliance of many

Reuters/Corbis-Bettmann

Amid overwhelming political and economic turmoil, Lieutenant General Prosper Avril grasped at the presidency in 1990, but the nation was already spinning out of control.

© Carol Halebian

Father Aristide (left) *entered the presidential race just two months before the election. Many people speculate that his last-minute announcement facilitated his defeat of the U.S.-backed candidate, Marc Bazin. But the country's hopes for new leadership were dashed in September 1991, when a military coup ousted the president-elect. The army again patrolled the streets* (below).

AP/Wide World Photos

political parties and organizations, officially sponsored Aristide's candidacy. But more important to Aristide than any political alliance was the support of the millions of people opposed to Duvalierism and to elite privilege. Aristide preached the need for a lavalas, a flood to cleanse the country of corruption. Through the lavalas movement, Aristide won the presidential election with over two-thirds of the votes cast. Bazin received only 14 percent of the ballots.

OVERTHROW AND RETURN

On January 16, 1991, just prior to Aristide's inauguration, the defeated Duvalierist candidate, Roger Lafontant, attempted to take over the government by force. Tens of thousands of people surrounded the presidential palace in support of Aristide, and Lafontant gave up. On February 7, 1991, Aristide was inaugurated as president of Haiti. Less than seven months later, however, the military, under Lieutenant General Raoul Cédras, threw Aristide out of office. Responding to international pressure, Cédras allowed

Raoul Cédras (on right) *and Aristide signed the Governors Island Agreement in July 1993, providing for the peaceful transition of power back to the elected president. The actual transfer happened more than a year later.*

Reuters/Fry Mages/Archive Photos

Aristide to fly into exile in Venezuela.

Although the OAS and the UN imposed arms and trade embargoes on Haiti to pressure Cédras to relinquish power, the economic and military sanctions did little more than create further hardship for Haiti's poor. Thousands of Haitians fled their homeland, most of them seeking to enter the United States as refugees.

While leaving the embargoes in place, the international community settled on negotiation as the primary means of resolving the conflict. The OAS and the United States led this effort. U.S. involvement was based on its role as the dominant political power in the Western Hemisphere, and its historic ties to Haiti following the U.S. occupation in 1915. The United States also desired to see the conflict resolved quickly before a flood of Haitian refugees attempted to enter the United States.

In July 1993, Cédras and Aristide signed an agreement at Governors Island in New York City. Under the agreement, Aristide was to appoint a new commander in chief to replace Cédras, who would retire before Aristide's return on October 30, 1993. But Cédras, the coup leader, was assigned to oversee the transition period, and those involved in the 1991 coup were promised a general **amnesty.** The Governors Island Agreement specifically requested UN personnel to assist in reforming the Haitian military and to supervise the establishment of a civilian police force. Aristide could name a new prime minister, picked from the business sector. In August Robert Malval and his cabinet were approved by the Haitian parliament. Afterward, in accordance with the agreement, the UN and OAS suspended the embargoes before Aristide returned. But, with the embargoes lifted, there was no incentive for Cédras and the military to follow through on their end of the deal.

As the date for Aristide's return neared, violence in Haiti escalated. In September 1993, a group called the Front pour l'Avancement et Progrès Haïtien (FRAPH, the Front for Haitian Advancement and Progress) emerged. FRAPH was a Duvalierist organization allied to the military. In a show of disapproval of Aristide, gun-carrying FRAPH members commemorated the anniversary of François Duvalier's inauguration on September 22 with a parade. On October 5,

More than 20 years after his death, François Duvalier's supporters still promoted his policies. Duvalierists protested in the streets during the months before Aristide's return, insisting on representation in the new government.

FRAPH supporters stopped U.S. embassy vehicles that had arrived to meet the USS Harlan County. FRAPH leader, Emmanuel Constant, later reported that he had collaborated with CIA members about the demonstrations.

Reuters/Corbis-Bettmann

FRAPH members, police, and paramilitary attachés attacked Senator Wesner Emmanuel, an Aristide supporter, and made an unsuccessful attempt to assassinate Port-au-Prince mayor Evans Paul.

On October 11, FRAPH turned out in force to meet the USS *Harlan County,* which had docked in Port-au-Prince with 200 Canadian and U.S. military instructors on board. The instructors were part of the UN advance team sent to Haiti as agreed in the Governors Island Agreement. A small number of FRAPH members and attachés waved guns and clubs, shouting, "No U.S. interven-

tion!" They also threatened visiting journalists and diplomats waiting to meet the contingent. Fearing danger to the soldiers on the ship, the United States ordered the ship back to its naval base at Guantánamo Bay. (Several reports have linked the CIA with having advanced knowledge of the FRAPH protest.)

The U.S. retreat was widely criticized in the UN and elsewhere, but back in the United States, public opinion strongly favored keeping the soldiers safe at all costs. In Haiti, however, the conflict was getting much worse. On October 14, 1993, Haitian Justice Minister François Guy

Malary was assassinated in front of the National Palace along with his driver and his bodyguard. All were killed by machine-gun fire from a passing vehicle. Malary had served under Aristide's prime minister Malval and had been insisting on the removal of a Supreme Court judge favored by the military. The assassination served to demonstrate the army's power. On the same day, heavily armed FRAPH members took parliament members hostage for more than an hour, demanding that Aristide reconcile with Cédras.

Cédras's tolerance of the violence and his prevention of a

UN presence made it clear that he would not honor the Governors Island Agreement. Aristide would not be returning to Haiti on October 30. Prime Minister Malval resigned on December 15, warning of a violent social upheaval to come. The UN and OAS embargoes were imposed again, and the United States braced for a renewed flood of refugees.

On July 31, 1994, the UN Security Council voted to oust Cédras by force. The Security Council authorized the formation of a multinational force that would use all means necessary to facilitate the departure of the military leadership in Haiti, to return President Aristide to office, and to restore Haiti's legitimate governmental authorities.

A 28-nation force, led by U.S. troops, landed in Haiti without opposition from the Haitian military on September 19, and President Aristide was returned to power. U.S. soldiers, expecting to land in hostile territory, had been told of a deal that President Carter had negotiated with leading Haitian generals and paramilitary authorities. In the hope of gaining cooperation from the military and

A year after the death of Justice Minister François Guy Malary (below), *U.S. troops* (above) *landed in Haiti with the overwhelming support of the Haitian public, who awaited the return of their president.*

Haitian demonstrators in Miami, Florida, protested the soft treatment the United States gave the leaders of the coup d'état that drove out Aristide.

of easing the transition back to civilian rule, Cédras and another coup leader, Colonel Philippe Biamby, were allowed to leave Haiti safely with their families on a U.S. military airplane. As part of the deal, they kept access to their fortunes, much of which had been embezzled from Haiti and deposited in U.S. bank accounts. In addition, the U.S. government leased Cédras's three homes in Haiti for thousands of dollars per month each, paying him six months in advance.

ATTEMPTS AT REFORM

Three years of military rule and international economic sanctions had left Haiti in even worse shape than it had been in after the departure of the Duvaliers. Aristide faced the dual tasks of establishing government control of the military and the police and of rebuilding the shattered economy.

The UN Mission in Haiti (UNMIH) was in place to help Aristide establish a secure and stable political environment. UN soldiers were to protect international personnel and key officials in case of another insurrection. The mission was also to assist in reshaping the Haitian armed forces and in the creation of a civilian police force. Its other task was to help the legitimate constitutional authorities of

Haiti in organizing fair and free elections.

The returning civilian government found Haiti's treasury empty and the army pension funds looted. Although Aristide's government opened complaint offices around the country to take reports of crimes committed during the coup, legal prosecutions did not follow. Even when police officers and others were arrested on charges of human-rights abuses, hundreds escaped or were quickly released from jails.

Port-au-Prince police chief Colonel Joseph Michel François, who played a leading role in promoting military violence against Haiti's citizens, fled to the Dominican Republic and then to Honduras, where he was granted **asylum.** Emmanuel Constant, the head of the paramilitary FRAPH death squad, fled to the United States. Although arrested by U.S. authorities, he was released against the wishes of the Haitian government. U.S. officials have said that returning him to Haiti would have a destabilizing effect on that country. In interviews Constant claims to have been offered asylum in the United States in exchange for his silence on his dealings with the CIA.

Reforming the corrupt, abusive military and police forces—a crucial step in rebuilding a secure and peaceful society—proved difficult. Upon his return to Haiti, President Aristide reduced the army from 7,700 troops to 1,500. In 1995 he disbanded the army altogether. Although 5,000 ex-soldiers took advantage of six months of vocational training and job placement help funded by the United States, many left the army with no jobs or resources. In 1996

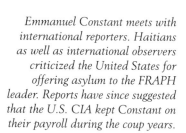

Emmanuel Constant meets with international reporters. Haitians as well as international observers criticized the United States for offering asylum to the FRAPH leader. Reports have since suggested that the U.S. CIA kept Constant on their payroll during the coup years.

Archive Photos

In 1995 hundreds of Haitians applied for the training program of the newly created police force.

Reuters/Carole Devillers/Archive Photos

groups of discharged soldiers attacked the Port-au-Prince parliament building and national police headquarters in retaliation. Others formed roving gangs of bandits, robbing and killing civilians and often ambushing police.

Aristide's plans also called for disarming the civilian attachés and other paramilitary organizations. However, no effective disarmament was ever carried out. Although U.S. officials placed high priority on disarming Haitian civilians, they were not will-ing to place this task in the hands of U.S. soldiers in Haiti. Former soldiers and attachés alike maintained their arsenals of grenades and automatic weapons. FRAPH members continued to threaten lavalas supporters, union activists, and human-rights workers. International human-rights groups, including Human Rights Watch/Americas and the National Coalition for Haitian Refugees, confirmed continuing abuse and murder by FRAPH and the attachés.

Creating a reformed Haitian National Police (HNP) proved no easier. Many former members of the military, police, and paramilitary organizations found their way into the new force. The police officers received four months of training through the International Criminal Investigations Training and Assistance Program, a project of the U.S. Federal Bureau of Investigation and the U.S. State and Justice Departments. But in the short term, the training proved insufficient to overcome entrenched habits of corruption and disregard for due process and other human rights.

By late 1996, more than 600 police officers were under investigation on charges of drug trafficking, armed robbery, and violations of human rights. By late 1997, more than 200 officers had been fired, and judges and prosecutors were also under arrest for involvement in criminal activity. The Platform of Haitian Human Rights Organizations, a nine-member coalition of human-rights groups, reported that most of the country still had no police presence and that drug and arms traffickers operated without difficulty.

Rebuilding the economy proved to be an even harder task. Haiti desperately needed the $1.2 billion that had been pledged in foreign aid. But to gain this money, President Aristide had to agree to certain economic policies mandated by foreign lenders. The U.S. Agency for International Development (USAID) and the Haitian government agreed to an $800,000 public relations campaign to convince Haitians that the proposed

> *. . . unlike almost every Haitian president who had preceeded him, Aristide did not seek to amend the constitution to extend his term.*

changes would lead to greater economic efficiency and, eventually, to economic growth. Nevertheless, Aristide proceeded slowly with the economic alterations, sensitive to the anger expressed by many of Haiti's citizens, who feared the reforms would only bring more hardship.

Aristide had little time to accomplish these goals because his term of office expired in January 1996. And, unlike almost every Haitian president who had preceded him, Aristide did not seek to amend the constitution to extend his term. Instead, Aristide and his government prepared to hold elections for a new president and legislature.

NEW ELECTIONS
UN workers assisted in preparations for the June 1995 legislative and local elections, as did various U.S. and foreign agencies. More than 400 foreign observers

supervised as Haitians chose among 10,000 candidates from 28 parties, all running for 2,200 offices. Despite many difficulties on election day, which included armed attacks on some candidates, the election was judged to be fair. Aristide's party, the Lavalas Political Organization (OPL by its French name), won a sweeping majority. Voter

© Daniel Morel/Sygma

René Préval—a member of the Lavalas Political Organization and backed by Aristide—became the second democratically elected president of Haiti.

participation in these elections, however, fell to about 50 percent, far below the 80 percent participation that had elected Aristide in 1990.

By the December 1995 presidential election, participation had fallen further, to only 15 percent. With the support of the OPL, former prime minister René Préval won the presidency. After the election, the OPL refused to back the economic changes agreed to by both Aristide and Préval. President Préval lost the support of his own party.

When Préval was inaugurated in 1996, he announced that efforts to **privatize** Haitian industries would be modeled on a plan adopted in Bolivia, a South American country. Under his proposed plan, the government would retain 50-percent ownership of state companies. Private investors holding the remaining 50 percent of company stock would make all business and operating decisions. Instead of paying the government for their 50 percent share, the private investors would use the capital to build up the companies and to make them more profitable. The government's share of the stocks would go into a fund to pay pensions to citizens when they retired.

This modified privatization plan met with opposition in the legislature and among the Haitian people, as did proposed layoffs of government workers and increased prices for food and fuel. Strikes and marches signaled popular dissatisfaction with the country's continuing economic problems. Préval found himself squeezed. He was under pressure from international lenders, without whose aid he would not gain the resources to rebuild the country. Similarly, Préval felt the pressure of domestic forces, without whose support the economic programs could not be implemented.

© Carol Halebian

Préval privatized (changed from state to private ownership) the Rice Corporation of Haiti, one of several government-run businesses. Foreign donors withheld millions of dollars of aid money until the plan had gone into effect.

Haiti and the United States

After 300 years of colonial rule, Haiti's first century of independence was tumultuous. Successive regimes each came to power by force. In 1915 the United States stepped in. By occupying Haiti, the United States could thwart foreign attempts to take advantage of political instability in the Caribbean as well as protect its stake in the newly opened Panama Canal.

The 19-year U.S. occupation of Haiti had several lasting effects. First, the U.S. military created the Gendarmerie d'Haïti that would become the modern-day army. Even after the occupation, the United States kept ties with Haitian officers, offering training and equipment. Second, the United States centralized economic and political power in Port-au-Prince, a move that weakened regional independence movements. Infrastructure improvements and trade incentives drew all trade to Port-au-Prince. This kept trade dollars away from other, minor ports. Third, the United States helped draft Haiti's first constitution. Its provisions eased trade and made Haiti economically dependent on the United States.

The United States supported the antidemocratic governments of the Duvaliers with money and military aid. In the 1950s, François Duvalier used the U.S. fear of Communism to gain support. The United States broke its ties to Haiti when Papa Doc's regime became openly oppressive. But in the 1970s, it supported Jean-Claude's government, which appeared less brutal and opened up trade. The United States and the international community stood by as foreign-aid funds went into the pockets of the president and the mulatto elite.

In the 1970s, foreign manufacturers took advantage of Haiti's low minimum wage, setting up 200 assembly plants. Rural people flocked to the cities. Foreign investors received large tax breaks from the Haitian government and made great profits selling their goods abroad. During a decade of apparent industrial development, workers' wages actually fell. In the 1980s, inflation, foreign debt, and unemployment were on the rise.

Seeing no improvements in human rights, the United States pulled its aid to Haiti and called for Jean-Claude to step down. The United States set up an interim government led by U.S.-trained Haitian officers and helped organize nationwide elections for 1990. Many experts believe the United States opposed the election of Aristide because he wanted to restructure the Haitian political system and was critical of the U.S. -Haitian policies.

After the 1991 coup, the U.S. and UN embargoes meant to punish Cédras's government. But numerous exceptions were made. The United States granted export permits to wealthy Haitian manufacturers. So, while the elite found ways to get around the embargoes, they hurt the poor majority of the Haitian people. Many suspect the United States of secretly supporting the coup and have criticized the country for its soft treatment of coup leaders.

Each successive Haitian government has had to agree to terms that increase Haitian poverty as they try to make payments on foreign loans. As the debt has grown, so has foreign, especially U.S., influence on Haitian economic policy. For the most part, this influence has not historically benefited the average Haitian citizen.

The public wasn't nearly so enamored of Préval as it had been with the charismatic Aristide. A resident of the seaside town of Jacmel held up a 1994 newspaper article about Aristide during a speech the ex-president gave in November 1996.

Lacking legislative approval of his economic programs, Préval's government ground to a halt. It could not agree on Haiti's annual budget. With no budget, redevelopment programs could not be enacted. With no legislative support for economic cutbacks, and lacking budgets to direct spending, international agencies held back redevelopment loans. Hungry and angry, the people took to the streets in protest.

By 1997 Haiti's infant democracy was paralyzed by political quarrels and was unable to make progress toward rebuilding the country. Meanwhile, Aristide announced the formation of a new political party, called the Lavalas Family. Aristide hinted that he might run for the presidency again in the year 2000 and said he would try to reunite the splintered coalition that had brought him to the presidency in

1991. But despite Aristide's hopes of renewing the country's faith in the political process, only 5 percent of registered voters turned out in April 1997 to vote for the thousands of positions on new local councils and to fill senate and chamber of deputies seats.

The election, moreover, emphasized that the groups that had once been united in support of Aristide and Préval could not resolve their differences. The OPL—which has since renamed itself the Organization of the People in Struggle to distance itself from Aristide—charged the Lavalas Family with electoral fraud in the April elections. Préval's prime minister, Rosny Smarth, resigned in June 1997 to protest the alleged rigging of legislative elections by Lavalas Family supporters. In June 1998, the OPL-controlled legislature refused to approve any of the candidates President Préval nominated to replace Smarth.

As the government remained paralyzed, a Haitian ferryboat ran aground and killed more than 70 people.

President Préval saw the disaster as a symbol of the desperate situation of his country. "It is the result of the dilapidation of the country," he said. "In 15 months, you can't do everything that was never done during 200 years. We are in a country in distress, and we don't know where it is all going to end." The fear is that it will end where it has repeatedly ended for Haiti—with another cycle of revolutions and violent coups. ⊕

A poll worker explains the ballot to a voter during local and legislative elections. Many Haitians have lost faith in the democratic process, after seeing their presidents ousted by coups and international powers dictate Haitian affairs.

AP/Wide World Photos

CHAPTER 5

WHAT'S BEING DONE TO SOLVE THE PROBLEM

After so many years of violence, most Haitians are desperate for peace and security. To establish the rule of law, the Haitian government hopes to permanently disband the paramilitary organizations, to disarm criminals, to reform the military and police, and to hold its officials accountable for their actions. It remains to be seen whether these tasks can be accomplished.

After decades of deprivation, Haitians yearn for jobs, schools, food, and housing. They are deeply divided, however, on whether the structural adjustment programs prescribed by international lenders offer a viable way to reach these social and economic goals. Will Haiti find a way to overcome its historic economic divisions? Where will the exhausted is-land find the resources to sustain a productive economy?

And what of Haiti's floundering electoral process? No democracy can sustain itself with only 5 percent of its citizens participating in elections. Can the deadlock between Haiti's executive and legislative branches be resolved peacefully? Can the democratic process in Haiti yield results that will restore the citizens' faith in the political process? These are questions that remain to be answered.

LAW AND ORDER

Serious problems within the HNP persist. Between January and October of 1997, police officers killed at least 46 people. Illegal searches and arrests are common, and police beatings continue at an alarming level. In addition, drug trafficking and general corruption related to the drug trade within the HNP ranks are believed to pose a serious threat to the integrity of the police force. Because of ongoing budgeting and administrative problems in the Haitian government, HNP officers are not paid regularly. This lapse makes the money from drug trafficking and other illegal sources harder to resist.

To help correct these persistent problems, the United Nations has maintained the UN Civilian Police Mission in Haiti. Nearly 300 police officers from 11 countries provide further training and monitoring for the inexperienced HNP. At least half of the UN officers are stationed

Canadian members of the UN Civilian Police Mission in Haiti oversee target practice of the Haitian National Police force.

UN/DPI Photo (187-35OC), by Eskinder Debebe

around the country, working closely with their Haitian counterparts. Another 12 to 15 foreign police officials working for the UN Development Program in Haiti are assigned to Haitian police units as advisers.

The HNP is much too small to serve a country of 8 million people, most of whom live in remote areas. Although nearly 500 new police officers began training in 1998, the force is only targeted to employ a total of 6,726 officers. This means that, for the majority of Haitians who live in the countryside, the nearest police officer may still be a full day's walk away.

Haitians, therefore, need alternative methods of conflict resolution, so that problems can be resolved before they reach the point that police intervention is needed. To this end, Peace Brigades International began a long-term project in Haiti. Peace Brigades teams work to train **justices of the peace,** human-rights workers, and ordinary Haitians in conflict resolution and conciliation techniques. The Joint Civilian Human Rights Mission of the UN and the OAS has participated in this project.

The first training session took place in the Artibonite Valley, north of Port-au-Prince. Many conflicts in the Artibonite Valley focus on the land, which is rich, well-irrigated, and valuable. Some friction arises from the traditional practice whereby farmers lend small plots to one another. This often leads to future questions of ownership. Other grievances are dominated by landowners whose political connections and financial resources allow them to bully their neighbors

CHAPTER 5 *What's Being Done to Solve the Problem* (89)

A Peace Brigades volunteer works with two Haitians during a role-playing activity during a conflict-resolution workshop. The program's critics, however, feel that such efforts do not address the real problems plaguing Haiti.

Peace Brigades International U.S.A

without fear of punishment.

The local leaders and justices of the peace attending the early training sessions doubted that the mediation techniques could help their situations. But a growing list of resolved conflicts has helped convince Haitian participants that these methods can actually work. In 1997, 20 Haitians who had attended Peace Brigades workshops formed a Haitian-run group called Rezolisyon Konfli (Conflict Resolution). The group collects information on emerging conflicts in the Cahos, a mountainous region northeast of the Artibonite River, and proposes remedies toward peaceful

resolution. Despite these efforts to attain peaceful solutions, conflict resolution doesn't get to the root of the real problems—gross economic and social inequality—plaguing Haiti.

ECONOMIC DEVELOPMENT

Large-scale efforts toward social and economic development depend on foreign assistance. The World Bank (an international organization, in connection with the UN, that provides loans to countries for development projects), the International Monetary Fund (IMF, an organization that provides short-term loans to 175 member countries), associ-

ated private institutions, and various foreign governments have all pledged their aid to Haiti. This international effort has focused its support on immediate poverty reduction, rebuilding the public sector, and laying the foundation for sustainable economic growth.

To this end, the World Bank coordinates and maintains several projects in Haiti. An example of the World Bank's approach is the renewal of La Saline, one of the dirtiest, poorest, and most dangerous slums in Port-au-Prince. In 1996 a Haitian government team and local residents discussed how to clean up and improve

La Saline. After talks with local associations, business-people, and residents, work began. The program is designed to drain open sewers, to rebuild enclosed sewer drains, to clean and repave the streets, and to create healthy open-air markets for the 500,000 people who crowd the neighborhood on market days.

The program is funded with $4 million from the World Bank's Road Maintenance and Rehabilitation Project. It uses local small- and medium-sized contractors and local labor to simultaneously address Haiti's chronic unemployment. Approximately 750 jobs have been created under the project.

Much of the money pledged to Haiti by the World Bank, the IMF, and other lending entities, however, is dependent on structural adjustments to Haiti's economic system. The adjustments include privatizing

> *Bowing to international and economic pressure, Préval's government has . . . agreed to push for privatization . . . .*

state-owned industries, increasing tax collection, removing price controls, and cutting government employment. In Haiti state-owned companies include the airport authority, the port authority, two banks, the cement company, the electric company, the vegetable oil company, the flour mill, and the telephone company. In the past, both Presidents Aristide and Préval opposed selling these companies to private investors. Bowing to international and economic pressure, Préval's government has since agreed to push for privatization in the form of joint private and government ventures. Under Préval's plan, government assets would remain under state control. Yet many Haitians still bitterly oppose privatization.

© Alyx Kellington/DDB Stock Photo

Residents of Cité Soleil work to clean up sludge in the neighborhood's sewers.

World Bank Projects In Haiti

The World Bank acts in cooperation with other international agencies and donor governments. The international donor community has pledged $2 billion in grants and loans to Haiti for 1995 to 1999. The World Bank estimates it will spend $390 million during this same time in its efforts to rebuild Haiti. World Bank projects in Haiti include the following:

© Carol Halebian

- The Water Supply Project provides drinking water for 225,000 people in Port-au-Prince.
- The Health and Population Project aims to improve health services to the poor and supports a national AIDS and tuberculosis program.
- The Economic and Social Fund, through the Haitian government, provides grants to grassroots organizations that quickly deliver basic social services to the poor.
- The Employment Generation Project creates short-term work for 325,000 poor Haitian men and women.
- The Power V Project provides investments in the power industry to ensure a reliable energy supply for industrial and commercial activities.
- The Industrial Recovery and Development Project provides financial and technical help to small- and medium-sized private industrial businesses.
- The Road Maintenance and Rehabilitation Project assists the Haitian government with its five-year road and bridge maintenance and rehabilitation program.
- The Basic Infrastructure Project will help rebuild the basic infrastructure in secondary cities, involving local communities, contractors, and workers. The project is designed to create long-term employment opportunities through construction and maintenance projects.

One reason for their opposition is that many of the people who have the money to buy into the companies are foreigners. Historically foreign ownership and the accompanying foreign influence have resulted in the net export of capital and resources, as well as challenges to Haitian sovereignty, and many fear a repeat of previous experiences. And although some Haitians are wealthy enough to buy the companies, they are the same members of the economic elite who own most of the country's productive resources already.

Unions representing workers in the state-owned companies also oppose the sales.

They fear that the companies' new owners would not honor contracts and would fire many workers. To make the companies more efficient and profitable, layoffs would be likely, adding to Haiti's unemployment problem.

As for the recommended cuts in government spending and public employment, the increased tax collection, and the end to price controls on food and fuel, the pain inflicted by these measures will fall heavily on Haiti's poor. Since the poor account for almost all of Haiti's population, opposition to these measures is widespread. Economists at the international lending institutions believe that the long-term benefit to the country's economy justifies the pain, but most Haitians remain unconvinced.

A draft of a 1996 World Bank strategy paper on Haiti revealed that rural farmers, who make up two-thirds of the population, will be unable to continue living off the land if the policies the bank advocates are adopted. According to the strategy paper, environmental constraints and low production volume will force many rural

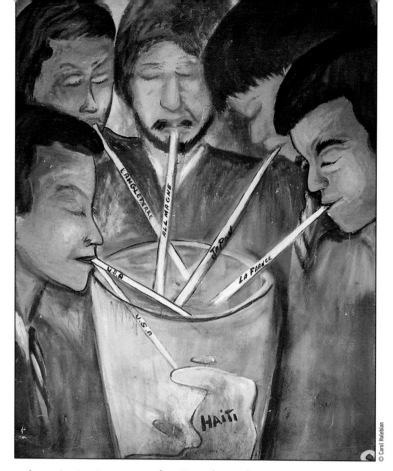

An anti-privatization mural in Haiti depicts foreign investors from the United States, Britain, Germany, Japan, and France drinking up Haiti's economy. Many Haitians oppose the privatization plan.

people into the cities to work in the industrial or service sectors. Haiti's overextended agricultural economy, already teetering on the brink of disaster, would be pushed over the edge. A massive and potentially destabilizing restructuring of Haitian society would result, with a mass migration of the rural poor into the already crowded cities in search of work.

Finding productive employment for Haitians, therefore, is a high priority. To this end, the Haitian government and international agencies are working to encourage both local and foreign investment in Haiti. One resource the country does

UN soldiers helped maintain order as frustrated jobless Haitians sought positions that the UN was offering. At that time, estimates showed that 70 percent of the population was unemployed.

factory, a bottled-water plant, a small cigar factory, and an essential-oils plant.

Many of those investing in Jacmel are Haitians or Haitian émigrés who fled to other countries and are returning. To encourage this kind of private investment, the Haitian Development Network (HDN) is seeking to educate potential investors about opportunities in Haiti. The HDN, a nongovernmental organization, hopes to tap into the skills and resources of the 2 million Haitian émigrés living abroad, as well as others interested in Haiti. The HDN believes that lasting economic development in Haiti must be based on trade and investment rather than on international assistance.

Even without substantial outside investment, however, Haiti has some established industries that have the potential for further development. Before the 1991 coup, for instance, exports of handicrafts earned between $10 and $15 million yearly. In Haiti, where jobs are scarce or nonexistent, money earned from basketmaking, wood carving, and other crafts is not supplemental in-

have is a large and willing labor pool.

When a UN-sponsored program offered jobs to build roads and bridges, so many applicants showed up that workers were hired for only two weeks at a time. That way, more people were given an opportunity for at least some employment. One Haitian man noted, with deep emotion, that it was the first job he had held in his life. He had always wanted to work, but had never had the opportunity.

The Haitian government's biggest job-development initiative so far is an $18 million project that joins public and private sectors with international donors to promote tourism, agriculture, and handicrafts in the seaside town of Jacmel, on the southern coast of Haiti. The USAID has agreed to repair the town's wharf, which would allow cruise ships to use Jacmel as a port of call. Private investors have plans for building a hotel in Jacmel, and others have recently opened a bank, an ice come but is the sole source of support for most artisans and their families. Various organizations strive to help these producers, most of whom work at home, earn still more for their crafts.

SERRV International, formerly known as Sales Exchange Refugee Rehabilitation and Vocation, is a nonprofit program that promotes the social and economic progress of people in developing regions of the world by purchasing and marketing their crafts. Unlike more commercial exporters, who pay producers as little as possible and keep the profits from sales, SERRV returns all profits to the local producers. Among SERRV's projects in Haiti are several artisans' cooperatives that produce art, handicrafts, and furniture from locally available materials.

In addition, there are several smaller-scale projects. These demonstrate that much can be accomplished without government or international lenders if the people directly affected by a problem get involved in its solution. In the Port-au-Prince slum of Delmas 32, for example, residents have joined together to provide safe and affordable drinking water, something Haiti's paralyzed government has largely failed to do. With help from the Research and Technical Exchange Group, an organization financed by the European Union (an organization of European countries devoted to economic growth), residents are building 11 fountains and 1 reservoir that will serve 50,000 people in the neighborhood. Since 1995 the group has helped local residents build 65 fountains in slums around Port-au-Prince, supplying 300,000 people with 30 percent of their water needs. Members of 14 neighborhood water committees are volunteers, but they employ more than 100 administrative workers and fountain attendants.

A craftsman displays a piece of oil-drum art. Some Haitians benefit from SERRV's program to support local artisans by selling their goods abroad.

A group of Haitians (above) mixes cement for constructing a school building in Cap-Haïtien. They are employed by Partners With Purpose, a Canadian-based humanitarian-aid group that raises funds for building projects and community rejuvenation.

Members of the Agriculturists Association meet in a town near Port-au-Prince. Perhaps the greatest hope for change in Haiti comes from the rural and urban grassroots organizations as people at the local level work to change their lives.

SOCIAL AND POLITICAL REFORM

Although Haiti is heavily dependent on foreign aid and assistance, much is done locally to improve Haitian society. The Ti Legliz (Little Church), the Central Workers Union, the National Federation of Haitian Students, and the National Popular Assembly provide ways for ordinary Haitians to affect the course of the country and their lives.

The Ti Legliz movement began in the 1970s, with the Catholic Church providing a place for farmers, workers, students, men, and women to come together to work for change. The Ti Legliz is not an organization with a formal structure. It is the name claimed by church people who share the same beliefs and work together toward social justice. Socially concerned church workers and members continue to be active in politics, preaching that love of one's brothers and sisters must be accompanied by action to make their lives better.

Unlike international lending agencies that dictate how and where their money is spent, grassroots organizations strive to enable Haitians in need, while maintaining their sense of dignity. Since Aristide's presidency, he has opened the Aristide Foundation for Democracy. The foundation started a bank that makes loans to small groups of women. As each member of the group repays her loan, another woman can borrow some money. The bank, modeled after the Gareen Bank in Bangladesh, India, has better chances of repayment, because the women share the responsibility of borrowing and paying off their loans.

Farming cooperatives and other rural groups first formed in the late 1960s and continue to seek land and greater rights for the people of the countryside. In addition to agricultural aid, they have also demanded tax reform to ease the burden on farmers. The Peasant Movement of Papay and the Tèt Kile Ti Peyizan (Small Farmers Put Their Heads Together) are among the leading rural organizations.

In urban areas, labor unions seek improved wages and working conditions. Unions, which operated underground during the Duva-

lier years, these days operate openly and have broadened their demands to include the protection of human rights. Numerous neighborhood committees also organize poor people to demand electricity, drinkable water, and protection against crime and police abuses.

While these popular movements may participate in electoral politics, many also rely on more direct actions to work toward their goals. All groups organize marches, demonstrations, and strikes. Peasant groups occupy land and demand title to it. With the country's apparent loss of faith in electoral politics, it is likely that these confrontational tactics will be used more often. It remains an open question what effect this will have on the nation's peace and stability.

The governmental paralysis that has gripped Haiti since late 1996 has jeopardized Haiti's prosperity. In 1997 the Haitian economy grew just 1.1 percent—much less than the 4.5 percent that had been projected. Much of the slowdown has been attributed to parliament's failure to pass the 1997 budget until late in the year. This re-

sulted in decreased government spending, which in turn resulted in less stimulation of the Haitian economy. In addition, much of the international aid that had been promised could not have been processed without a fully functioning government, and serious investors were scared off.

The ongoing governmental paralysis also threatened the electoral process, leading to the postponement of scheduled November 1998 elections. These elections were to have been for members of the entire lower chamber of the parliament, as many as 66 percent of Senate members, and all local officials.

The stalemate among the various political factions may be a sign that, for those who would govern Haiti, little has changed. How this problem may be solved remains to be seen. But if the economic and political crises do not move toward resolution, the consequences for Haiti are predictable. If Haiti cannot establish a system of government that responds to the needs of the people and the nation, then the poverty and violence that have nearly destroyed the country will inevitably continue. ⊕

EPILOGUE*

By the end of the 1990s, the Haitian government was at an economic and political standstill. After Rosny Smarth's resignation in June 1997, the power struggle continued. The OPL-controlled parliament refused to approve four prime minister candidates proposed by Préval, a member of the Lavalas Family. Moreover, the parliament did not approve any of the Préval government's budgets. The continuing political and economic instability scared off foreign investors, and international lending agencies held back foreign aid, costing the country hundreds of millions of dollars in much-needed funds.

In January 1999, Préval, resentful of the uncooperative parliament, planned to appoint a new government. He disregarded parliament, saying the terms of most elected members had run out. Parliamentary elections, which had been repeatedly postponed, provided no new members who could assume seats in the legislature. Demonstrators, frustrated with the government standoff, marched in support of the president's decision to override the legislature. Préval proposed to appoint a provisional electoral committee to arrange and to oversee parliamentary elections. However, international bystanders feared that Préval's move would end democracy in Haiti. Meanwhile, the Haitian population has shown its distrust of the government by its failure to vote in elections.

At the same time, accusations have surfaced against members of the Haitian National Police for violating human rights and for participating in the illegal drug trade. Dwindling government funds have dampened the spirits of the small police force. Complicating Haiti's future is the potential withdrawal of the 400 U.S. troops stationed in Haiti. Although Préval has not approved the withdrawal, the departure of U.S. troops and other international personnel could have a negative effect on the struggling HNP.

*Please note: The information presented in *Haiti: Land of Inequality* was current at the time of the book's publication. For late-breaking news on the conflict, look for articles in the international section of U.S. daily newspapers. The *Economist*, a weekly magazine, is another good source for up-to-date information. *The Miami Herald* publishes frequent reports about Haiti, which you can access via the Internet through HERALDlink, an online version of the newspaper. The address is http://www.herald.com/americas/carib/haiti/. Also try "This Week in Haiti," the English abstract of *Haiti Progrés*, a Haitian newsweekly. The Haiti Information Bureau in Port-au-Prince publishes a biweekly newspaper in English called "Haiti-Info." For a subscription, write to hib@igc.apc.org/. For more links, contact Haiti News and Links at http://www.greatbasin.net/~networth/haiti/news.htm/.

CHRONOLOGY

1492 Columbus lands at Môle St. Nicolas, on the northwest tip of Hispaniola.

1697 The Treaty of Ryswick divides the island of Hispaniola between the French in the west and the Spaniards in the east.

1789 The French National Assembly accepts a mulatto petition of rights in October.

1790 In October, Ogé leads a mulatto uprising in northern Saint Domingue.

1791 The voodoo priest Boukman leads a ceremony in the woods of Bois Caïman on August 14. On August 22, the slaves revolt. In the months that follow, over 10,000 slaves and 2,000 French are killed. Many of the surviving whites return to France, leaving behind over 1,000 ruined plantations.

1793 On August 29, the French commissioner Sonthonax declares the slaves free. On the same day, Toussaint-Louverture calls on the noir rebels to follow him.

1797 Sonthonax appoints Toussaint commander in chief of the French forces.

1798 In October the remaining French troops are forced to sail for France.

1799–1800 War of Knives. Toussaint leads his noir forces against the mulattoes in southern Saint Domingue, who are led by Rigaud, Pétion, and Boyer. The noir victory is followed by the killing of between 5,000 to 10,000 mulattoes.

1801 In January Toussaint's handpicked assembly drafts a new constitution and declares Toussaint governor-general for life.

1802 France tries to regain control of Saint Domingue. In June Toussaint is betrayed and sent to France, where he dies in prison.

1804 Dessalines declares Haitian independence on January 1. From January until March, virtually all of the remaining French are massacred.

1806 Revolt against Dessalines, who is betrayed and killed on October 17.

1807 In the north, Christophe proclaims himself president of the State of Haiti. In the south, Pétion is elected president of the Republic of Haiti. Six years of civil war follow.

1818 Death of Pétion. In the south, Boyer is elected president for life.

1820 On October 8, Christophe commits suicide when he learns his men are marching against him. Boyer immediately marches north with his troops and reunites Haiti on October 26.

1825 France agrees to recognize Haitian independence on the condition that Haiti pay 150 million francs in compensation.

1838 France grants Haiti final and complete independence.

1843 Boyer overthrown.

1848 On April 16, Soulouque directs a massacre of mulatto leaders in Port-au-Prince.

1867 Start of the Cacos Revolts, as peasants in the north demand land and better economic conditions.

1883 La Semaine Sanglante, September 22–25. The noir president, Salomon, orchestrates a massacre of as many as 4,000 mulattoes.

1915–34 The United States occupies Haiti, takes control of the Haitian National Bank and customhouses, dissolves the army, and imposes a new constitution.

1957 François Duvalier is elected president. The voting is marred by widespread fraud and military intimidation.

1964 Duvalier declares himself president for life.

1971 Duvalier dies and is succeeded by his son, Jean-Claude, who continues his father's repressive practices.

1986 On February 7, Jean-Claude Duvalier is forced to give up power and fly into exile. The National Council of Government assumes control of Haiti, but many officials from the Duvalier regime retain power in a period known as "Duvalierism without Duvalier."

1987 A week before the November 29 election, Namphy names himself head of the armed forces for the next three years. Election day violence is widespread.

1988 Namphy schedules a second election for January, which is boycotted by most opposition groups. Namphy later deposes the winnner, Manigat, but is himself overthrown by Avril in September.

1990 Avril is sent into exile, and Aristide announces his candidacy for president.

1991 Aristide is inaugurated as president of Haiti on February 7. On September 30, Cédras overthrows Aristide and sends him into exile. The OAS imposes an embargo on October 7. In November the U.S. Coast Guard forcibly returns the first of many boatloads of Haitian refugees.

1993 The UN imposes an embargo on June 16. In July, Cédras and Aristide sign the Governors Island Agreement, calling for a list of reforms and setting a date for Aristide's return. Cédras violates the agreement in October.

1994 In July the UN votes to allow an invasion of Haiti to remove the military regime. On September 19, the United States leads the invasion. Cédras goes into exile, and Aristide returns to power.

1995 In December René Préval is elected president, but only 15 percent of voters participate in the elections.

1996 Aristide announces the formation of a new political party, the Lavalas Family, and hints that he will run for the presidency in the year 2000.

1997 Only 5 percent of voters turn out for the April elections, and the OPL accuses the Lavalas Family of election fraud. In June Prime Minister Smarth resigns. The crisis brings virtually all government action to a standstill.

1998 The political crisis paralyzes the government. The legislature, dominated by the OPL, repeatedly refuses to approve any of the candidates President Préval nominates to fill the position of prime minister.

SELECTED BIBLIOGRAPHY

Abbott, Elizabeth. *Haiti: The Duvaliers and Their Legacy*. New York: Simon and Schuster, 1991.

Aristide, Jean-Bertrand with Christophe Wargny. *Aristide: An Autobiography*. Translated by Linda M. Mahoney. Maryknoll, NY: Orbis Books, 1993.

Aristide, Jean-Bertrand. *In the Parish of the Poor: Writings from Haiti*. Translated and edited by Amy Wilentz. Maryknoll, NY: Orbis Books, 1990.

Danticat, Edwidge. *The Farming of Bones: A Novel*. New York: Soho Press, 1998.

Danticat, Edwidge. *Krik? Krak!* New York: Soho Press, 1995.

Deren, Maya. *Divine Horsemen: The Living Gods of Haiti*. London and New York: Thames and Hudson, 1953.

Farmer, Paul. *The Uses of Haiti*. Monroe, ME: Common Courage Press, 1994.

Greenberg, Keith Elliot. *A Haitan Family*. Minneapolis: Lerner Publications Company, 1998.

Greene, Graham. *The Comedians*. New York: Viking Press, 1966.

Haiti in Pictures. Minneapolis: Lerner Publications Company, 1995.

James, C.L.R. *The Black Jacobins: Toussaint Louverture and the San Domingo Revolution*. London: Allison and Busby, 1980.

North American Congress on Latin America. *Haiti: Dangerous Crossroads*. Edited by Deidre McFayden, et. al. Boston: South End Press, 1995.

Roumain, Jacques. *Masters of the Dew*. Translated by Langston Hughes and Mercer Cook. Introduction by J. Michael Dash. London: Heinemann, 1978.

Schmidt, Hans. *The United States Occupation of Haiti, 1915–1934*. New Brunswick, NJ: Rutgers University Press, 1971.

Steber, Maggie. *Dancing on Fire: Photographs from Haiti*. Introduction by Amy Wilentz. New York: Aperture Foundation, 1991.

Trouillot, Michel-Rolph. *Haiti, State against Nation: The Origins and Legacy of Duvalierism*. New York: Monthly Review Press, 1990.

Wilentz, Amy. *The Rainy Season: Haiti since Duvalier*. New York: Simon and Schuster, 1989.

INDEX

ABOUT THE AUTHOR

A freelance writer and former attorney, Mary C. Turck has degrees in law (Loyola University of Chicago), religious studies (University of St. Thomas), and psychology (University of Chicago). She writes for and edits a monthly news review covering Latin America and the Caribbean for the Resource Center of the Americas and a monthly newsletter covering hemispheric trade issues for the Institute for Agriculture and Trade Policy. She has written numerous books for young readers, including books on Guatemala, Mexico, and Honduras. Ms. Turck lives in St. Paul, Minnesota, with her husband, Ron Salzberger, and two daughters, Molly and Macy.

ABOUT THE CONSULTANTS

Andrew Bell-Fialkoff, *World in Conflict* series consultant, is a specialist on nationalism, ethnicity, and ethnic conflict. He is the author of *Ethnic Cleansing*, published by St. Martin's Press in 1996, and has written numerous articles for *Foreign Affairs* and other journals. He is currently writing a book on the role of migration and the history of the Eurasian Steppe. Mr. Bell-Fialkoff lives in Bradford, Massachusetts.

Catherine Orenstein is an independent journalist who has lived in and reported on Haiti on and off since 1990, when she received a Peabody-Gardner fellowship from Harvard University for a year of research there. In 1995 and 1996, she investigated crimes against human rights for the United Nations Civilian Human Rights Mission and for the Haitian government.

SOURCES OF QUOTED MATERIAL

p. 24 Aristide, Jean-Bertrand with Christophe Wargny. *Dignity*. Introduction by Christophe Wargny. Translated and with an afterword by Carrol F. Coates. (Charlottesville, VA: University Press of Virginia, 1996), 6; p. 25 Aristide, Jean-Bertrand with Christophe Wargny. *Dignity*. Introduction by Christophe Wargny. Translated and with an afterword by Carrol F. Coates. (Charlottesville, VA: University Press of Virginia, 1996), 58; p. 36 James, C.L.R. *The Black Jacobins: Toussaint Louverture and the San Domingo Revolution*. (London: Allison & Busby, 1980), 43; p. 37 James, C.L.R. *The Black Jacobins: Toussaint Louverture and the San Domingo Revolution*. (London: Allison & Busby, 1980), 38; p. 42 Quoting François-Dominique Toussaint-Louverture, "Declaration of Camp Turel" speech. Trouillot, Michel-Rolph, *Haiti, State against Nation: The Origins and Legacy of Duvalierism*. (New York: Monthly Review Press, 1990), 43. p. 44 Ibid; p. 46 Ibid; p. 58 Abbott, Elizabeth. *Haiti: The Duvaliers and Their Legacy*. (New York: McGraw-Hill, 1988), 41; p. 61 Abbott, Elizabeth. *Haiti: The Duvaliers and Their Legacy*. (New York: McGraw-Hill, 1988), 70; p. 64 Abbott, Elizabeth. *Haiti: The Duvaliers and Their Legacy*. (New York: McGraw-Hill, 1988), 87; p. 91 Ibid.